ASIL Studies in International Legal Theory

The purpose of the ASIL Studies in International Legal Theory series is to clarify and improve the theoretical foundations of international law. Too often the progressive development and implementation of international law has foundered on confusion about first principles. This series raises the level of public and scholarly discussion about the structure and purposes of the world legal order and how best to achieve global justice through law.

This series grows out of the International Legal Theory project of the American Society of International Law. The ASIL Studies in International Legal Theory series deepens this conversation by publishing scholarly monographs and edited volumes of essays considering subjects in international legal theory.

Books in the series

The Authority of International Criminal Law: A Controversial Concept Clare Frances Moran

The Death Penalty's Denial of Fundamental Human Rights John Bessler

Theories of International Responsibility Law Edited by Samantha Besson

Human Dignity in International Law Ginevra Le Moli

Tipping Points in International Law: Commitment and Critique Edited by Jean d'Aspremont and John D. Haskell

Ethical Leadership in International Organizations: Concepts, Narratives, Judgment, and Assessment Edited by Maria Varaki and Guilherme Vasconcelos Vilaca

Whither the West?: Concepts on International Law in Europe and the United States Edited by Chiara Giorgetti and Guglielmo Verdirame

International Law as Behavior Edited by Harlan Grant Cohen and Timothy Meyer

THE AUTHORITY OF INTERNATIONAL CRIMINAL LAW

Despite a wealth of literature exploring the issues surrounding it, the legitimacy and authority of international criminal law remain in question. Adopting a perspective informed by legal and political philosophy, Clare Frances Moran considers the authority of international criminal law, why it can be conceived of as more than simply an exercise of power and how that power may be exercised legitimately. Advancing existing scholarship on the subject, Moran explores the roots of the authority of law at the domestic level and tests these ideas in an international context. She examines sovereignty, complementarity, and postcolonial issues, and how each impacts international criminal law. By developing a theory on the authority of international law, Moran considers how it might be possible to adjudicate more effectively at the international level.

Clare Frances Moran is Lecturer in Public International Law at the University of Aberdeen, where she teaches and researches international criminal law. She has held visiting positions at Columbia Law School and the Max Planck Institute for Foreign and International Criminal Law.

Space and Fates of International Law: Between Leibniz and Hobbes Ekaterina Yahyaoui Krivenko

Why Punish Perpetrators of Mass Atrocities?: Purposes of Punishment in International Criminal Law Edited by Florian Jeßberger and Julia Geneuss

The Challenge of Inter-Legality Edited by Jan Klabbers and Gianluigi Palombella

The Nature of International Law Miodrag A. Jovanović

Reexamining Customary International Law Edited by Brian D. Lepard

Theoretical Boundaries of Armed Conflict and Human Rights Edited by Jens David Ohlin

Human Rights in Emergencies Edited by Evan J. Criddle

The Theory of Self-Determination Edited by Fernando R. Tesón

Negotiating State and Non-State Law: Global and Local Legal Pluralism Edited by Michael A. Helfand

Jus Post Bellum and Transitional Justice Edited by Larry May and Elizabeth Edenberg

Normative Pluralism and International Law: Exploring Global Governance Edited by Jan Klabbers and Touko Piipaerinen

The Future of International Law: Global Government Joel P. Trachtman

Morality, Jus Post Bellum, and International Law Edited by Larry May and Andrew T. Forcehimes

Global Justice and International Economic Law: Opportunities and Prospects Edited by Chios Carmody, Frank J. Garcia, and John Linarelli

Parochialism, Cosmopolitanism, and the Foundations of International Law Edited by M. N. S. Sellers

The Role of Ethics in International Law Edited by Donald Earl Childress III

The New Global Law Rafael Domingo

Customary International Law: A New Theory with Practical Applications Brian D. Lepard

International Criminal Law and Philosophy Edited by Larry May and Zachary Hoskins

The Authority of International Criminal Law

A CONTROVERSIAL CONCEPT

CLARE FRANCES MORAN
University of Aberdeen

CAMBRIDGE
UNIVERSITY PRESS

CAMBRIDGE
UNIVERSITY PRESS

Shaftesbury Road, Cambridge CB2 8EA, United Kingdom

One Liberty Plaza, 20th Floor, New York, NY 10006, USA

477 Williamstown Road, Port Melbourne, VIC 3207, Australia

314–321, 3rd Floor, Plot 3, Splendor Forum, Jasola District Centre, New Delhi – 110025, India

103 Penang Road, #05-06/07, Visioncrest Commercial, Singapore 238467

Cambridge University Press is part of Cambridge University Press & Assessment, a department of the University of Cambridge.

We share the University's mission to contribute to society through the pursuit of education, learning and research at the highest international levels of excellence.

www.cambridge.org
Information on this title: www.cambridge.org/9781108483650

DOI: 10.1017/9781108678629

First published 2023

A catalogue record for this publication is available from the British Library.

A Cataloging-in-Publication data record for this book is available from the Library of Congress

ISBN 978-1-108-48365-0 Hardback

For J.F.L. and E.S.L.

Contents

Preface

The creation of courts and tribunals, and the undertaking of trials at the international level, has often been argued to lack legitimacy. The charges levelled range from claims of victors' justice and postcolonial bias to arguments that individual courts lack jurisdiction or have been created to further the interests of certain powerful States. Whatever foundation these claims may (or may not) have, the creation of a system of international criminal justice remains an act of power. Its legitimacy should be of concern to all, yet the question of how legitimacy might be assessed has not been fully explored. As a term, legitimacy is frequently mentioned in the literature concerning international criminal law, and specifically that which focuses on the International Criminal Court, as well as being a common theme in other areas of international law. The debate, however, remains limited in nature: for international criminal law, the focus has been squarely on the question of whether the International Criminal Court possesses legitimacy, without considering how this may be defined or elaborated. Legitimacy in international criminal law remains critically understudied. A closer look at the concept of legitimacy in general reveals its connections to the idea of authority which, as will be demonstrated in this work, precipitates legitimacy. Authority, unlike legitimacy, is rarely mentioned and only recently has attracted more attention in international law scholarship. The contents of these concepts and their connection to power require further investigation.

Accordingly, this book attempts to reframe the debate by looking at the concept of legitimacy through the lens of authority. Specifically, it examines what authority constitutes and how this affects legitimacy. This argument focuses on asking a certain set of questions: what sort of authority does the International Criminal Court have? What is meant by authority? How does this concept link to power and legitimacy?

The three concepts – legitimacy, authority, and power – are intrinsically connected, and in no area more closely than international criminal law. This book centres on the question of whether international criminal law, as an area of law, constitutes a legitimate exercise of power. There has been repeated questioning of the legitimacy of international criminal tribunals,[1] the hybrid war crimes tribunals during the Second World War,[2] and, more recently, the International Criminal Court.[3] Legitimacy arises as a question because of the lack of a central State authority in international criminal law, and public international law generally. The agreement on which the international system is predicated is not necessarily the only requirement for the creation of mechanisms of international criminal justice and, indeed, sometimes it is not required at all. The question of legitimacy, however, rarely goes beyond the mention of the word: there are few discussions of what legitimacy means in international law and fewer yet of how the system of international criminal justice might secure legitimacy. The focus on whether the system has legitimacy also ignores a deeper look at the links between legitimacy, authority, and power. This book is an attempt to remedy that deficit and to refocus the problems faced by international criminal justice on the issue of its authority.

1 See, among others, Nobuo Hayashi and Cecilia Baillet, *The Legitimacy of International Criminal Tribunals* (Cambridge University Press 2017); Laura A Dickinson, 'The Promise of Hybrid Courts' (2003) 97 AJIL 295; Antonio Cassese, 'The Legitimacy of International Criminal Tribunals and the Current Prospects of International Criminal Justice' (2012) 25 LJIL 491.

2 Guénaël Mettraux (ed), *Perspectives on the Nuremberg Trial* (Oxford University Press 2008); Neil Boister and Robert Cryer, *The Tokyo International Military Tribunal: A Reappraisal* (Oxford University Press 2008); Yuma Totani, *The Tokyo War Crimes Trial: The Pursuit of Justice in the Wake of World War II* (Harvard University Press 2009); Alexander Sukharev, 'The Nuremberg Tribunal and the Problems of International Rule of Law' (2006) 77 RIDP 711.

3 Catherine Gegout, 'The International Criminal Court: Limits, Potential and Conditions for the Promotion of Justice and Peace' (2013) 34 TWQ 800; Mandiaye Niang, 'Africa and the Legitimacy of the ICC in Question' (2017) 17 ICLR 615.

Acknowledgements

I am immensely grateful for the support I have received from many individuals and organisations, without whom this work would never have reached completion. The funding from the Carnegie Foundation for the Universities of Scotland and the Society of Legal Scholars allowed me to take up a visiting scholarship at Columbia University, New York. Columbia provided generous resources and an excellent environment in which to develop and write the manuscript. The editorial staff at Cambridge encouraged and supported the work from an early stage and throughout the review process. My thanks and gratitude go to Tom Randall for his unwavering support and consideration during the submission process. The reviews he sought made the work far better than it could have been with my input alone. I am very grateful to the critical efforts of the reviewers, who have generously given their time and consideration of my ideas. My thanks also go to Joao de Sousa Assis and Thomas Moran for reading through the manuscript at various stages, and my mother, Frances Moran, for her skill as my informal editor and her presence as dedicated grandmother.

My thanks go to my parents and my brother for their endless encouragement and kindness. I am so grateful to my husband, Joe, for all his support throughout my academic career. It would be a very different experience without him.

Any errors in the work remain mine alone.

1

Introduction

When the International Criminal Court (the ICC/the Court) released a warrant for the arrest of Sudanese President Omar al-Bashir in 2009, the response from political world leaders and their advisers was mixed. The responses from States[1] ranged from enthusiastic support for the ICC, and thus acknowledgement of its authority and jurisdiction as a court, to tacit rejections of its independence and its ability to effect justice for the victims of the crimes, to complete disregard for it as an institution. The French and British Foreign Offices welcomed the decision, while the Russian Special Envoy to Sudan and the Senegalese President expressed their displeasure with the Court. al-Bashir's own response was that the ICC could 'eat' the warrant.[2]

The response of al-Bashir is not uncommon from those who are accused of international crimes: the defendants indicted before the tribunals at Nuremberg submitted a motion arguing that their prosecution was against the established principle of no crime without law.[3] The defence counsel on behalf of Tadic's[4] case before the International Criminal Tribunal for the former Yugoslavia (ICTY) submitted a motion questioning the authoritative jurisdiction of the Tribunal.[5] Although both motions were rejected by the respective courts, the intention to query the jurisdiction of such a court indicates that the courts are

1 'Sudan: Reaction to Warrant for Bashir's Arrest' *Thomson Reuters*, 4 March 2009, https://reliefweb.int/report/sudan/sudan-reaction-warrant-bashirs-arrest.

2 'Sudanese President Tells International Criminal Court to "Eat the Arrest Warrant"' *The Guardian*, 4 March 2009, www.theguardian.com/world/2009/mar/04/sudan-al-bashir-war-crimes.

3 Nullum crimen, nulla poena sine lege; Motion adopted by Defense Counsel, 19 November 1945, Nuremberg Tribunal 1945, see http://avalon.law.yale.edu/imt/v1–30.asp#1. See Kirsten Sellars, 'Imperfect Justice at Nuremberg and Tokyo' (2010) 21 EJIL 1085–1102; Stanley Paulson, 'Classical Legal Positivism at Nuremberg' (1975) 4 Phil & PA 132–158.

4 *Prosecutor v Tadic* IT-91-1.

5 Decision on the defence motion on jurisdiction 10 August 1995, *Prosecutor v Tadic* IT-91-1.

not accepted by all, particularly those who are defending themselves before them, as authoritative arbiters of international criminal law. This gives rise to an argument regarding the authority and legitimacy of international criminal tribunals. Much has been written about the problems of the legitimacy of such institutions,[6] and the debate regarding the legitimacy of the ICC has been particularly strong in recent years. This has been compounded by the fact that the practice of the Court has lent credence to the arguments of potential bias which might undermine legitimacy: every individual indicted by the ICC has been African, and that no powerful Western leaders have been the subject of the Court's attention. Despite this, the debate tends to centre on the reasons for the lack of legitimacy or attempts to provide solutions for the Court's lack of legitimacy. The underlying problem of what would constitute legitimacy or authority for the Court is rarely explored.[7] This problem is exacerbated by the lack of discussion of the links between authority and legitimacy in international criminal law, and how this may affect the perception of the authority of such institutions. Given the practical impact, which can be seen in the above examples, of the ICC lacking authority and legitimacy, the discussion of such problems is a critical area for research. This work seeks to deal with the issue by exploring the concept of authority and seeking to provide a theory of authority of international criminal law. The overarching intention of the work is to contribute to a more focused debate on the reasons for the Court's perceived and actual lack of legitimacy.

1.1 THE AUTHORITY OF LAW: DOMESTIC SYSTEMS AND CRIMINAL LAW

Before turning to the authority of international criminal law, the discussion of the authority of law more generally should be considered, beginning with the work of Joseph Raz. Raz has contributed extensively to the debate on authority and considers the concept of authority to be one of the most controversial

[6] See, among others, Karen Alter, Lawrence Helfer and Mikael Madsen, *International Court Authority* (Oxford University Press 2018); Nobuo Hayashi and Cecilia Baillet, *The Legitimacy of International Criminal Tribunals* (Cambridge University Press 2017); Catherine Gegout, 'The International Criminal Court: Limits, Potential and Conditions for the Promotion of Justice and Peace' (2013) 34 TWQ 800–818; and Mandiaye Niang, 'Africa and the Legitimacy of the ICC in Question' (2017) 17 ICLR 615–624.

[7] Allen Buchanan, 'The Legitimacy of International Law', and David Luban, 'Fairness to Rights: Jurisdiction, Legality and the Legitimacy of International Criminal Law' both in John Tasioulas and Samantha Besson (eds), *The Philosophy of International Law* (Oxford University Press 2010).

which exists in legal (and political) philosophy.[8] Its controversy is linked to the fundamental issue of determining what authority is and how it may underpin certain acts and rules. Although it may be considered controversial, an understanding of authority is critical to understand why the law has any power over individuals in society, at both the domestic and international levels. This is particularly important at the international level because of the significant power that some States possess in comparison to others. However, it does not stand alone as a concept: the question of the authority of law is intrinsically linked to that of legitimacy. Legitimacy, in the context of political systems, requires the authority of that system to be recognised by other actors.

The idea of legitimacy tends to be discussed within theories of the right to rule, or justifications for governments. From this debate, there is often reference to authority, although it is discussed in varying degrees of depth by legal and political theorists: Mill wrote that authority and liberty were competing values, that a tension existed between the two, but did not divulge his own conception of authority or breach the discussion further. His writing tends to focus instead on the existence of a government which then has the power to rule, within certain limits, and there is no inkling that the ideas of power and authority should be separated.[9] The command theory, propagated by John Austin, requires a command backed by a sanction without explaining why the State possesses authority in the first instance to command its subjects.[10] Instead, he focuses on the power the State has. Austin shares some similarities to Mill, in that they both refer to the power of the sovereign, its might, rather than any authority it may possess. Interestingly, Austin notes that, were everyone sufficiently 'competent,' all individuals in society could be sovereign.

Weber takes a different view and defines authority in terms of whether a directive will be obeyed.[11] He links, in his discussion, the concepts of power and authority to the legality of a political order, offering a perspective on what may constitute authority. He conceptualises authority as belief, which he regards as pertinent for the legitimacy of the system. This perspective remains political, rather than legal, although it does shed some light on the authority of legal systems. From a legal theory perspective, Raz and Kelsen have posited that the authority of law may emanate from different sources. Kelsen focuses

8 Joseph Raz, *The Authority of Law* (1st edn, Oxford University Press 1979), 3.

9 John Stuart Mill, *On Liberty* (first published 1859, Dover Publications 2002).

10 John Austin, *The Province of Jurisprudence Determined* (first published 1832, General Books 2012).

11 Max Weber, 'The Three Types of Legitimate Rule' (1958) 4 Berkeley Pub Soc Inst 1.

on his famous 'basic norm'[12] on which law's authority may be founded. Raz, alternatively, makes the argument that authority exists because the law is a legitimate exercise of power.[13] The idea of authority is developed to the greatest extent by Joseph Raz. Although not cited directly, it is a further development of Weber's idea of authority founded on belief in the system as legal and legitimate, and leading on to identify that there is no requirement for individuals to follow the law. Instead, he posits that the law possesses authority to the extent that it supports individual autonomy.[14]

These conceptualisations of authority provide a useful, although not exhaustive, explanation of authority at the domestic level. Inherent in their understanding of authority is the presence of a domestic government. These conceptualisations also explain why individuals in domestic societies should obey the law, and detail why such law ought to be considered to have authority. The domestic criminal system is thus rationalised by such theories: as Weber notes, individual faith in the domestic criminal law is explained through the criminal proscription of activities which most individuals would consider harmful. As Raz notes, domestic criminal law is also justified because of its protective function against general harm for the population as a consequence of its deterrent function.

These theories, however, have not been examined in the context of international law and it remains to be seen as to whether these arguments would stand up to scrutiny in respect of international criminal law. Despite the idea of international criminal law as an extrapolation of domestic criminal law,[15] it lacks a sovereign or central authority which could demand compliance. There is also a lack of connection to the individual, meaning that the argument that it could serve individual autonomy through obedience to rules cannot be considered, as the individual has little engagement with the creation and even the operation of the system. Although the conceptualisation of authority is important at the domestic level, it has much greater complexity and consequence at the international level because the international system lacks a centralised body or institution which governs all States. The capacity of States to create international law and to accept its constraints raises interesting questions, such as from where the authority derives and how it permits States to create international legal rules which can be described as legitimate.

[12] Hans Kelsen, *Pure Theory of Law* (2nd edn, The Lawbook Exchange 2005).

[13] Joseph Raz, *The Morality of Freedom* (Oxford University Press 1988).

[14] ibid.

[15] MC Bassiouni, 'The Permanent International Criminal Court' in M Lattimer and P Sands (eds), *Justice for Crimes against Humanity* (Bloomsbury 2003), 181.

1.2 PUBLIC INTERNATIONAL LAW AND ITS AUTHORITY

The question of public international law's authority and legitimacy thus requires some consideration before examining the authority of international criminal law, which exists as part of the wider discipline of public international law. Public international law broadly exists as a set of legal rules created by States and, historically, there has been some discussion on the authority of public international law. Grotius, among others, argued that the authority of the State and its right to govern stemmed from the agreement of its polity.[16] This agreement forms the foundation of State authority at the international level, which would then mean that international law may derive its authority from the States which create the rules, although Grotius did not discuss the idea any further. In contrast, Vitoria focused on individual reason as the basis for authority: his concept was that the natural law and natural order must be respected by others where an organising system such as States or groups existed.[17] His central contribution was to undermine the universality of papal authority, meaning that the idea of authority was more closely drawn to natural law and reason than to the divine order. However, he did not offer any conclusions as to why international law ought to have authority: the discussion of reason and its impact on authority at the international level would have to have been discussed in greater detail.

Other authors have also given the idea their attention more recently. Kelsen's legal theories have been applied to public international law by von Bernstorff.[18] Çali[19] also discusses the use of consent as the source of the authority of international law, arguing that authority in international law is intrinsically linked with the authority of domestic law. Other authors have also regarded the importance of the State, such as Criddle and Fox-Decent.[20] They jointly argue for the recognition of States as the organisations which safeguard rights, as the way in which the international system can function legitimately. Teitel[21] also argues for the existence of an order beyond statehood which restricts the ability of States to act and protects rights in international law.

16 Hugo Grotius, *Commentary on the Law of Prize and Booty* (Oxford University Press 1950).

17 Francisco de Vitoria (ed AR Pagden and Jeremy Lawrance), *Vitoria: Political Writings* (Cambridge University Press 1991).

18 Jochen von Bernstorff, *The Public International Law Theory of Hans Kelsen: Believing in Universal Law* (Cambridge University Press 2010).

19 Başak Çali, *The Authority of International Law: Obedience, Respect and Rebuttal* (Oxford University Press 2015).

20 Evan J Criddle and Ewan Fox-Decent, *Fiduciaries of Humanity: How International Law Constitutes Authority* (Oxford University Press 2016).

21 Ruti Teitel, *Humanity's Law* (Oxford University Press 2011).

Autonomy is key in the eyes of Besson as the source of international law's authority,[22] while Franck's work on legitimacy[23] supports the idea that the law is obeyed by States when legitimate, and, accordingly, the law has greater authority when legitimate.

These authors set out interesting arguments regarding both authority and legitimacy in the context of international law. A central limitation remains in that it is difficult to apply any of these ideas to international criminal law. Despite the links between public international law more broadly and international criminal law, including similarities in terms of principles, sources and in other ways, there is a key difference: international criminal law is a direct constraint on both individual and State autonomy without necessarily requiring the consent of either the State who may have jurisdiction over the crime or the individual who has been indicted. The central function of criminal law, in restraining behaviour, makes international criminal law significantly different from other branches of public international law. In the same vein, the Rome Statute permits a referral of a non-State party to be made by the UN Security Council (UNSC). This, in and of itself, has the power to undercut the requirement of State consent, through an investigation of the behaviour, or acts within the jurisdiction of, non-State parties.[24] Accordingly, a different approach to analysing its authority must be undertaken.

1.3 AUTHORITY AND LEGITIMACY IN INTERNATIONAL CRIMINAL LAW

The authority of international criminal law raises different questions from that of general international law, and yet the issue has not been dealt with in much detail. Considerations of authority tend to abate in favour of discussions on whether international criminal law in general imposes victors' justice, or whether there exists bias, primarily that which is postcolonial in nature. The scholarship which examines the law of the ICC tends to focus on analysing the law itself[25] and there is little discussion on the purpose of the Court

[22] Samantha Besson, 'The Authority of International Law – Lifting the State Veil' (2009) 31 Sydney LR 343.

[23] Thomas Franck, *The Power of Legitimacy among Nations* (Oxford University Press 1990).

[24] Luigi Condorelli and Annalisa Ciampi, 'Comments on the UNSC Referral of the Situation in Darfur to the ICC' (2005) 3 JICJ 590 and Dapo Akande, 'The Legal Nature of Security Council Referrals to the ICC and Its Impact on Al-Bashir's Immunities' (2009) 7 JICJ 333.

[25] Otto Triffterer (ed), *Commentary on the Rome Statute of the International Criminal Court* (Beck Hart Nomos 2008); Roy Lee (ed), *The International Criminal Court: The Making of the Rome Statute* (Kluwer Law International 1999); Ilias Bantekas, *International Criminal Law* (Hart 2010); and William Schabas, *The International Criminal Court: A Commentary on the Rome Statute* (Oxford University Press 2010).

generally, as it tends to be presumed. There is very little on the authority of international criminal law beyond the Court once questions of victors' justice were presumed to be resolved or of little further interest. Questions regarding the legitimacy of international criminal law are not new,[26] but there has been a greater concentration on questions of the Court's authority and legitimacy over the past few years.[27] As there is no overarching theory of authority posited for this area of the law, questions regarding authority and the legitimacy of the ICC will continue to be raised, which may have a damaging impact on the future of the Court. There are two specific areas which affect the authority of international criminal law, and the Court as the central vehicle for its enforcement. These are complementarity and UN Security Council referrals to the ICC.

Unlike other international criminal tribunals, the ICC has neither primary nor exclusive jurisdiction. Instead, its jurisdiction is complementary to that of national courts. In the context of the ICC, it may prosecute where the State is 'unwilling or unable genuinely'[28] to undertake prosecution. The doctrine of complementarity allows the principal obligation to prosecute to rest with the State, meaning that the authority remains with the State until such time as they cannot or will not exercise their right to do so. Any investigation by the ICC would be predicated on evidence, to an extent, that the 'unwilling or genuinely unable' test was satisfied, typically due to an extensive delay in prosecuting individuals[29] or a clear attempt to protect individuals from prosecution.[30] This creates a further step in the Court's admissibility threshold;[31] it may only proceed if there is no reasonable possibility of prosecuting at the domestic level.[32] Complementarity acts as a bulwark against the exercise of universal jurisdiction[33] by the Court, differentiating the ICC system to an extent from broader international criminal law. Domestic authorities must be

[26] William Schabas, 'Victor's Justice: Selecting "Situations" at the International Criminal Court' (2010) 43 JMLR 535.

[27] See, among others, Alter et al. (n 6); Hayashi and Baillet (n 6); Gegout (n 6) 800–818; and Niang (n 6) 615–624.

[28] Article 17(1)(a), Rome Statute. *See* Carsten Stahn, 'A Tale of Two Notions of Complementarity' (2008) 19 CLF 87.

[29] Article 17(2)(b), Rome Statute.

[30] Article 17(2)(a), Rome Statute.

[31] Article 1, Rome Statute. *See also* William Schabas, 'Complementarity in Practice: Some Uncomplimentary Thoughts' (2008) 19 CLF 5.

[32] *See Prosecutor v Saif Al-Islam Gaddafi and Abdullah Al-Senussi* ICC-OI/II-OI/IIOA6, 24 July 2014.

[33] Olympia Bekou and Robert Cryer, 'The International Criminal Court and Universal Jurisdiction: A Close Encounter?' (2007) 56 ICLQ 49.

given the opportunity to prosecute, and, in the absence of compelling reasons, the Court may not attempt to exercise universal jurisdiction over all States.

In international criminal law more generally, States are permitted to prosecute individuals under universal jurisdiction on the proviso that there exists domestic or international law criminalising the conduct. The ultimate power to prosecute rests with the State and the purpose of universal jurisdiction remains in line with that of the ICC: to ensure that there is no impunity for international crimes by providing a forum for prosecution. However, the authority to do so is difficult to parse: some States make ample use of universal jurisdiction,[34] while others have instigated very few prosecutions, such as the United Kingdom. The authority to do so appears to be derived from the State power to prosecute domestically and to honour international obligations. Consequently, its authority for such acts connects directly to the constitutional settlement of the State, as opposed to anything beyond the State.

The second way in which complementarity, and the question of authority, is complicated, is via the provision of a referral mechanism which can be used to self-refer, refer other States to the ICC[35] or for the UN Security Council to make a referral.[36] This can be used as an alternative to both universal jurisdiction and domestic prosecution for nationals of the State itself.[37] Under article 13(b) of the Rome Statute, the UN Security Council is empowered to refer a situation to the ICC, justified by its Chapter VII mandate to maintain peace and security, while article 14 permits the State to refer a situation to the ICC, including one within its own borders.[38] Although a deeper exploration of this and the reasons therefore are beyond the scope of this particular work, it has complicated matters where the Court's commitment to complementarity has been questioned.[39]

34 Maximo Langer and Eason Mackenzie, 'The Quiet Expansion of Universal Jurisdiction' (2019) 30(3) EJ IL 779.

35 Article 14, Rome Statute; *see also* Darryl Robinson, 'Inescapable Dyads: Why the International Criminal Court Cannot Win' (2015) 28 LJIL 323; Steven Roper and Lillian Barria, 'State Cooperation and International Criminal Court Bargaining Influence in the Arrest and Surrender of Suspects' (2008) 21 LJIL 457.

36 Condorelli and Ciampi (n 24) 590 and Akande (n 24) 333.

37 Each of the situations in Mali, the Central Africa Republic, and Uganda were referred by the individual governments.

38 Ahmed Samir Hassanein, 'Self-referral of Situations to the International Criminal Court: Complementarity in Practice – Complementarity in Crisis' (2017) 17(1) ICLR 107–134.

39 James Gondi, 'Debunking the Conspiracy Theory: Analysing the Failure to Achieve Complementarity and the Responsibility to Protect in Kenya and Other Jurisdictions' in Steve Ndirangu, Edigah Kavulavu and Terry Jeff Odhiambo (eds), *International Criminal Justice: The ICC and Complementarity* (ICJ Kenya 2014).

Thus, the connection between the State and the ICC goes beyond questions of jurisdiction: it derives its authority, its legitimate power to act, from the authority that States possess to create treaties, such as the Rome Statute. The creation of treaties by consent demonstrates one of the main sources of authority in international law: the consent of States. The treaty, and the rules thereunder, have authority because the States possess the authority to create the treaty in the first place. It would then appear reasonably straightforward: The States Parties have given their agreement to the laws under the Statute and so the Rome Statute has the power to act within the jurisdiction of these States in a manner complementary to the domestic system. As part of this complementarity, States Parties must also be 'unwilling or unable genuinely' to prosecute,[40] meaning that national prosecution must be given the opportunity to prosecute first. This places the primary responsibility for prosecution on the State.[41] However, this mechanism complicates the question of authority, because of the potential accusations of abuse of power or politically motivated referrals.[42] Such power complicates the question of the Court's authority: without a clear conception of authority in international criminal law, the Court may be viewed *in aeternum* as a vehicle for the values of the powerful, rather than universal values. International law in general is vulnerable to the influence of economically and politically emboldened States:[43] with the ICC, international criminal law may also be vulnerable to abuse by those with neo-colonial intentions. From where authority is derived requires further exploration to evaluate the basis for such claims.

1.4 THE PATH THIS TEXT WILL TAKE

Authority has been explored as a concept which is controversial in nature[44] because of the way in which it justifies the exercise of constraints on actions and limitations on behaviour. In a legal sense, this would usually connect to the idea of jurisdiction, particularly in relation to criminal law, because of the way in which it requires individuals to conform to or abstain from certain conduct. Authority has been explored to an extent by certain theorists, who note the struggle between freedom, autonomy, and authority, and who have sought to analyse the concept in a way which makes sense, to understand the

40 Article 17(1)(a), Rome Statute of the International Criminal Court 1998 (hereafter: Rome Statute).

41 Article 1, Rome Statute.

42 Robinson (n 35) 323, 327.

43 See Philippe Sands, *Lawless Word: Making and Breaking Global Rules* (Penguin 2006).

44 Raz, *The Authority of Law* (n 8) 3.

existence of freedom in tandem with the existence of rules. To that end, authority relates to both political and legal spheres; the work of Joseph Raz can be used as a useful bridge between the two areas.

The key arguments in this book are set out in six substantive chapters which explore each of these facets in turn. The first substantive chapter addresses this tension by discussing what is meant by authority and focuses on the work of both legal and political theorists to support an understanding of the concept. The relevance of autonomy is considered, and the links between authority and power are also discussed, before turning to an appreciation of the idea of legitimacy. The distinctions between the two ideas, as well as their connections are detailed before the discussion concludes with an analysis of authority and legitimacy in the context of criminal law. This is used to determine whether the restraints placed on autonomy in this context can ever be considered legitimate, and thus whether there is an issue with the authority of domestic criminal law.

Chapter 3 then examines the role of authority in public international law, based on the preceding discussion of authority and legitimacy in the context of exercises of power. Although there is a source of power, if not authority, at the domestic level in the form of government, this does not automatically transfer to the international level. This is primarily because the international system exists without a central authority. The question automatically arises of who ought to be able to make such rules, and whether the requirement for the exercise of autonomy is still as critical as it would be at the domestic level. The discussion is based on an analysis of foundational texts, exploring the ideas of authority at the international level expounded by Grotius and Vitoria, before moving to work by more recent authors. The importance of humanity and the guiding principle of protecting individuals as authority are explored, to identify potential issues for authority in the context of international criminal law created by such approaches. The issue of State consent looms large; for public international lawyers, the focus on voluntary consent is critical, but it is considered as to whether this may undermine the authority of international criminal law where State power may not be exercised legitimately.

The fourth chapter then proceeds to the idea of authority in international criminal law. Although there are links between international criminal law and public international law, rooted in the treaty agreements which created the former, the partly compulsory nature of international criminal law sets it apart from other forms of public international law. The drafting of the Rome Statute has had a specific impact on the nature of international criminal law because there is now a permanent international court which may try serious violations of international criminal law. It has also codified crimes and defences, and sets out the jurisdiction of the Court. Accordingly, this chapter focuses on the way in which the Rome Statute's jurisdiction, as its primary exercise of power and, potentially, authority, is set out in the treaty and how this may affect its authority. As its jurisdictional provisions also permit the UNSC to make referrals to the Court, where a situation threatens international peace and security, the question of this power going beyond 'typical' jurisdictional powers will be discussed in the context of power politics. This will allow an exploration of the mechanism as a legitimate exercise of power.

This chapter concludes the first part of the book, which considers what is meant by authority at the domestic and international levels, as well as specifically within international criminal law. The second part to the book considers challenges and a proposed theory of international criminal law. These include the question of sovereignty and the use of complementarity and the question of the postcolonial context. The hybridised moral authority and political power which has created the Court would also appear to guide it, which may, in certain cases, undermine its authority.

The first chapter in the second half of the book, Chapter 5, examines the interaction between sovereignty and complementarity. It deals with an analysis of both concepts, including the political idea of 'sovereignty costs,' in which powerful actors will commit to actions which limit their power to achieve overarching aims. The exercise of complementarity in both postcolonial States and wealthy, Western States will also be examined to determine whether such exercises of complementarity undermine the Court, or if these could reinforce the Court's authority.

The issue of shielding, as a natural corollary to the preceding discussion, will then be analysed, taking the examination of the situation in the UK/Iraq as a prime example. Shielding, as the protection of citizens from international prosecution through obfuscation, faux domestic trials, or the tacit or open refusal to provide available evidence, will also be explored in the context of preventing prosecution for those accused of serious violations of international criminal law. This serves as a precursor to a discussion of the examination of Afghanistan, which may confront the same issues and should be considered given that the UK/Iraq examination by the Court has now been concluded. This is then developed to question whether the sovereignty of more powerful States, such as the UK, holds greater weight than that of less powerful States. As a question, this remains critical for international criminal law, primarily because of the effect this asymmetry would have on the authority of the Court, and international criminal law more generally. The recognition that votes and vetoes count for more should they be cast or used by certain countries is problematic for the Court, where it seeks to end impunity, enforce the rule of law, and provide justice for victims where there is little prospect for justice otherwise. As such, its mission and impact are at particular risk where such an effect can be demonstrated.

Chapter 6 then begins to shape the theory of authority posited by this book, by exploring the way in which the authority of international criminal law is rooted in both justice and rights, exploring the development of international criminal justice in parallel with the human rights movement, and the way in which both have sought to serve victims of abuses. It also explores the way in which a reliance on State consent as the source of authority can undermine the authority of international criminal law. This argument is underpinned using Third World Approaches to International Law (TWAIL) scholarship. Such scholarship offers the opportunity to move away from the Euro- and State-centric approach to international criminal law and encourages a greater focus on domestic prosecution. If the true aim is to end impunity, a more complete approach to complementarity should be undertaken. The discussion engages with what this complete approach should comprise, exploring the impact of generalised support for domestic prosecutions to ensure that its exercises of power are truly legitimate, and that its aims are fulfilled at both the international and the national level.

The final substantive chapter sets out the results of the preceding discussion in the form of a theory of authority. The original idea underpinning this project was that the authority of international criminal law should be viewed as circular, where the authority flows from the consent of States through international law and back to the States themselves. The second conception was, initially, of international criminal law as a series of principles. Neither conception has weathered the research undertaken; the postcolonial context did not support such an understanding. A relationship with State consent may be possible in the future, but it derides the project of international criminal justice as impartial because of its reliance on the support of States which have caused such historic damage in postcolonial spaces.

Drawing on the previous discussion of postcolonialism, the State, and the ability of the UNSC to make referrals to the Court, the argument will be put forward that these remain an unstable, and potentially destabilising, foundation on which to base authority. The lack of a clear basis requires a different theoretical approach. The next part to the discussion looks at the idea of authority rooted in both justice and rights, discussing the development of international criminal justice alongside the human rights movement, and the way in which the justification for following such rules is rooted in an understanding of the rules serving the international population, particularly those vulnerable to atrocity crimes and victims of previous crimes. The last part to the chapter looks at the implications for a theory of authority based on rights for areas such as positive complementarity and UNSC referrals, and how these areas may need to adjust to conform to an understanding of authority which supports the legitimate exercise of power in this area. As is frequently noted, the Court's main aim is to end impunity. If this is truly the case, it should move towards a complete approach to complementarity. This completeness should involve the generalised support for domestic prosecutions to ensure that its exercises of power are truly legitimate, and that its aims are fulfilled at both the international and the national level.

2

The Link between Authority and Legitimacy

2.1 INTRODUCTION

As mentioned before, authority has been characterised by Joseph Raz as one of the most 'controversial concepts in legal (and political) philosophy.'[1] His perspective on its controversy is based on the idea that it is difficult to understand what is meant by authority, even by those who have it, and those who are subject to it tend to give it scant consideration,[2] despite the power it gives to rule-makers over their lives. This makes its controversy quiet in nature, as most do not think about the authority exercised over them, and only when the roots of authority are examined does it become contentious. The concept of authority relates to questions such as how law binds its subjects, and whether certain rules ought to be followed. Critically, it mandates an examination of the justifications the rule-makers have in exercising power to make rules.

This is important at all levels of rule-making, but particularly so in respect of domestic criminal law, because of the way in which criminal law requires individuals to adhere to a certain level of conduct. There is no element of consent to criminal law, unlike other areas such as contract law, meaning that it has a direct impact on the autonomy of the individual. These restrictions, such as they are, have a direct impact on individual autonomy with the aim of protecting the vulnerable and securing society in respect of crimes against the person. Although it is acknowledged that criminal law regulates a variety of conduct, the focus here is on crimes against the person because of its relevance to much of the conduct proscribed under international criminal law. Authority, autonomy, and legitimacy will be explored in detail in this chapter, to explain the justifications for the exercise of authority in respect of domestic criminal law.

1 Joseph Raz, *The Authority of Law* (1st edn, Oxford University Press 1979), 3.
2 Hannah Arendt, *Between Past and Future: Six Exercises in Political Thoughts* (Viking 1961), 91.

The first part to the discussion relates to authority and the approaches to the concept by political and legal theory. Analyses of authority are conducted to varying extents by legal and political theorists. John Stuart Mill notes that there is a tension between authority and liberty but does not outline a conception of authority. He tends to focus on the fact that governments have the power to rule, within limits, but does not distinguish power from authority.[3] Austin's command theory identifies the way in which law coerces its subjects via power, but does not explain the State's authority to do so.[4] He argues instead that the sovereign's power, rather than its authority, is the source of its ability to do so and tacitly suggests that were all individuals sufficiently competent, sovereignty may rest with each individual. Weber takes a more realistic view of authority, based largely on political authority, by stating that it is the likelihood that a directive will be obeyed.[5] He links power and authority to the existence of a legal order, meaning that belief in the system allows orders to be imposed on the population.

The writing of Joseph Raz provides a critical link between the more political discussions of authority and those of legal authority, as he identifies the significance of the political system to the concepts of authority, freedom, and legitimacy.[6] He notes that there are three forms of authority: one can be an expert, one can have the right to do something, or one can have the right to grant the permission to do something.[7] The common thread binding every one of these ideas is the exercise of power: one has the power gained from the recognition of one's expertise, one has the power to act, or one has the power to permit others to act. He clarifies the conception further in respect of political authority, to distinguish it from the exercise of power alone: to exercise authority, you need to have the right to command[8] and de facto power.[9] Authority is a direct result of the need to be governed and therefore there must be a right to rule,[10] along with requisite limitations, since untrammelled authority to act cannot be considered legitimate.[11] From this perspective, there are several ideas at the heart of authoritative rule creation and

3 John Stuart Mill, *On Liberty* (first published 1859, Dover Publications 2002).

4 John Austin, *The Province of Jurisprudence Determined* (first published 1832, General Books 2012).

5 Max Weber, 'The Three Types of Legitimate Rule' (1958) 4(1) Berkeley Pub Soc Inst 1.

6 ibid 1, 1.

7 Joseph Raz (ed), *Authority* (Basil Blackwell 1990), 1.

8 Ibid 2.

9 ibid 3.

10 ibid 5.

11 ibid 12.

decision-making: the idea of legitimacy; the idea of authority and how it interacts with autonomy; and the idea of power. The purpose of this chapter is to separate out these ideas, as best as possible, and to identify their connections to one another, to better understand what is meant by having authority.

The first part to this discussion analyses the concept of authority, using the work of legal and political theorists, exploring how authority goes beyond the idea of exercising power. The second will provide an analysis of autonomy, to appreciate its relevance to the idea of authority. The third will explore the concept of legitimacy, again with reference to both legal and political theory. Each section will work to provide a fundamental understanding of the concepts before demonstrating how they connect to one another. The conceptualisations of authority provided by both legal and political theorists will be explored here in detail, to offer a deeper understanding of both approaches. This will lay the groundwork for a deeper exploration of the use of power in international criminal law later in the book and, ultimately, to examine the authority of international criminal law as a legitimate exercise of power.

2.2 THE CONCEPT OF AUTHORITY

Both political and legal theorists have taken some interest in the idea of authority, although there is not a great deal of detailed discussion of the concept beyond one or two authors. Older theories, or those which rest on historical analyses, focus on authority as an exercise of power. These understandings of authority might relate to the existence of a sovereign, or to the likelihood that those issuing the instructions will be obeyed. Other political conceptions examine how power is transferred. The first characterisation of authority explored here is authority which is synonymous with the sovereign government or vested therein.

Traditional legal theorists undertook an observational approach to authority, examining the societies in which they lived and accounting for the exercise of power by those who made the law. As such, authority stemming from a government, sovereign, or command structure is embraced by both Mill and Austin. Command theory, as set out by Austin, requires a sovereign, a central body, or an individual with the power to rule, who can then issue instructions and sanction those who disobey. It is very much predicated on the exercise of power as a key determinant of authority,[12] which authorises the right to rule or to command.[13] Thus, the subjects of the sovereign do not tend

[12] Mill (n 3).
[13] Austin (n 4).

to question the instructions given to them as authority has been predetermined by the possession of power. There is no further examination of the roots of authority beyond power by either author, nor an examination of how power might be gained or removed, or the right to rule assessed. The existence of the sovereign in such cases is deemed sufficient for the legitimate exercise of power, which makes it difficult to assess the roots of its authority. The existence of a sovereign almost makes the discussion of authority moot; obedience is commanded. The question then arises of who or what the sovereign might be: Austin identifies it as the 'superior' person or body which is in the habit of creating rules,[14] distinguishable from subjects and their consequent inferiority by the fact that the latter is in the habit of following the set rules. His focus on authority is very much on power, although there is an allusion to the idea that sovereignty could rest with every individual in society were they sufficiently competent.

However, his approach does not tend to stray from observations of how monarchies and governments behave, founded on the Hobbesian premise that the authority is rooted in the ability of the lawmaker to create rules on a continuous basis, and that the rules accordingly remain law.[15] Not much more detail is offered beyond this; reference is made to the authority of the government and the possibility that it could relate to the constitution, but there is little discussion of why that may be. This arises as a theme in other work considering the authority of political power: Arendt's work traces the origin of authority back to the power of the Roman patres, who 'authored'[16] their system of government and acquired their power through descent. She wrote that 'the authority of the living was always derivative, depending upon the . . . authority of the founders, who no longer were among the living. Authority, in contradistinction to power . . . had its roots in the past.'[17] They possessed the ability to command because of their position, which was typically linked to their family. Any argument concerning their authority would be entirely circular because their power stems from their position, which then stems from their or their family's power, and so forth.

It should be noted here that this was not Arendt's final view on authority, but rather her observations on how authority operated in this context. Although both approaches correctly observe political and legal machinations in both British and Roman societies, there is still little exploration or critique

[14] ibid 165–166.
[15] ibid.
[16] Arendt (n 2) 121–122.
[17] ibid 122.

of this authority. Indeed, both accept the existence of authority when the sovereign or ancestral tie is identified, and possibly acknowledge that a failure to comply would result in the imposition of a sanction. Both conceptions detail who has the position of power, and who may wield it, but not whether they can exercise that power in an authoritative fashion. Later conceptions of authority indicate that the acceptance of a command theory or the absolute rights of sovereign government is slightly outdated from a legal perspective,[18] and tends not to be as common among more modern theorists. Hart, for example, judges the command theory to be 'threadbare'[19] because of the absence of a connection to morality, but not because the government or ruler lacks authority. However, his idea that command theories as such require further elaboration is indicative of their failure to develop the notion of authority beyond the identification of who possesses power, and to regard compliance as anything more than the consequence of an exercise of power.

Thus, historically, the individual who or institution which possessed power also had authority. The power connoted the ability to make decisions and create rules, and there was an expectation, coercive or otherwise, that the rule will be followed. In a system where power and authority are synonymous, obedience is expected as the sovereign (or patres) holds the power to impose a sanction. This expectation of obedience is interesting because it connects the traditional view of authority with a more modern conception: the connection between commands and obedience, which is of greatest interest if we wish to move beyond the idea that power and authority are simply synonyms, and to understand how authority works in systems which espouse democratic values. Raz[20] and Wolff[21] explore to a greater extent the connection between commands, obedience, and authority, recognising that compliance must be something other than the consequence of an exercise of power. Both consider the ability to command as a key aspect of both authority and power but have taken a much more detailed approach to the idea of how authority is exercised when a command or directive is issued.

Raz, in fact, offers a definition of what he considers authority to mean. He acknowledges that power is a requirement of authority,[22] and notes that there

[18] HLA Hart, 'Separation of Law and Morals' 17–37 in Ronald M Dworkin (ed), *The Philosophy of Law* (Oxford University Press 1977), 20.

[19] ibid 19.

[20] Raz, *Authority* (n 7) 2.

[21] RP Wolff, 'The Conflict between Authority and Autonomy' 20–31 in Joseph Raz (ed), *Authority* (Basil Blackwell 1990), 20.

[22] Raz, *Authority* (n 7) 3.

may be no initial distinction between power and authority.[23] Authority, in his view, can take three forms: expertise, a prerogative, and the power to grant permission.[24] Although the first form of authority, as a specialist, would not tend to be viewed as a form of political or legal power, it would be disingenuous to ignore the power that recognised expertise grants to those who possess it. The latter forms of power are much more recognisable examples of normative power in which an individual may act because of the authority he or she possesses. Political authority thus engages the prerogative and the power to grant permission through a right to command[25] and de facto power.[26] Wolff also acknowledges that authority is connected to a command but develops the idea further in that there should be an expectation that commands are followed.[27] This expectation of obedience supports the idea that there is a right to rule[28] which is held by the individual in possession of power. However, this is not to say that this right is limitless; there are certain constraints on the right to rule as untrammelled authority to act cannot be considered legitimate.[29] The idea of legitimacy will be considered in greater detail later in this chapter once a general exposition of authority has been made.

Raz's concept can thus be summarised as authority being the right to give an order, and to expect that order to be followed.[30] In this way, there are two key elements to Raz's concept of authority: the ability to act and the reasonable expectation that any directives given should be followed. Thus, the distinction between power and authority becomes clearer: it is not only the ability to issue the directives, but the expectation that they will be respected by others. It is thus authority as the 'ability to perform certain kinds of actions,'[31] and, centrally, to change the reasons for which individuals act. His work rejects the idea that the law commands and holds instead that the power is exercised to effect change in reasons for behaviour. This is outlined well by Wheatley, who notes that Raz's thesis describes those who have authority[32] as those who are accepted as having that authority with a grouping of individuals

23 Raz, *The Authority of Law* (n 1) 18.

24 Raz, *Authority* (n 7) 1.

25 ibid 2.

26 ibid 3.

27 Wolff (n 21) 20.

28 Raz, *Authority* (n 7) 5.

29 ibid 12.

30 Raz, *The Authority of Law* (n 1) 22–24.

31 Raz, *Authority* (n 7) 7.

32 Steven Wheatley, 'A Democratic Rule of International Law' (2011) 22 EJIL 525, 532–533.

who recognise and follow the directives given. This develops the idea of authority as relating to the rights of those who respect it: indeed, those who were subjects under the command theory are considered, under this approach, autonomous beings who can recognise the authority of those who issue directives. The right to rule should thus be justified in line with the autonomy of individuals to recognise authority. In this way, Raz links the ideas of political and legal authority, because of his recognition that power exercised through force, with the veil of authority, is not a sufficient account for authoritative action.[33] It must be followed, or obeyed, by individuals who recognise the authority as such.

Other modern theorists concur. Weber detaches from the idea that commands are issued and notes that authority is where a directive is likely to be obeyed. His discussion connects the ideas of power and authority to the existence of a system or legal order, characterising the likelihood of following the directive as connected to the belief in the system. This links well with the work of Raz, who also concludes that individuals do not need to obey the law. This approach is almost demanded of modern positivists, and other legal theorists, who seek to make sense of legal-democratic systems in which freedom and autonomy are key aspects, and which do not accept that individuals can be violently coerced into obedience under the guise of authoritative action.

Dworkin takes a similar view, in that validity[34] of the act is distinct from the authority of the directive: the rule-maker should have authority,[35] but their acts will only continue to have authority if the population accepts them as such.[36] Although he does not explore authority in any more depth, it highlights another dimension to authority which has been discussed by both Arendt and Raz. The idea of compliance cannot be merely connected to the exercise of power; it must go beyond the rule-maker's power and relate to the autonomy of the individual, if it is to truly reflect how democratic societies operate. As such, Arendt's idea of the command is relevant here because of the division she makes between power and authority: for authority, there should be no external means of coercion. In her eyes, where there must be resort to force, the exercise of authority has failed.[37] She further posits that authority

33 Raz, *Authority* (n 7) 3.

34 Ronald M Dworkin, 'Is Law a System of Rules?' 38–65 in Ronald M Dworkin (ed), *The Philosophy of Law* (Oxford University Press 1977), 41.

35 ibid.

36 ibid.

37 Arendt (n 2) 92–93.

and freedom are directly connected,[38] although acknowledges that there is a link between force and authority: the end result from the exercise of both is the same, in that people obey, but one has legitimacy while the other does not.[39]

The idea of legitimacy is therefore critical for authority as an exercise of power. It goes beyond mere consent, which would reinforce authority,[40] and requires that authority, both 'justified' and 'effective,'[41] be a legitimate exercise of power. Thus, legal authority should be justified in its exercise to be legitimate, and justification may often be found in the necessity for action.[42] From Raz's perspective, the extent to which the law has authority corresponds to whether it serves the individual's autonomy.[43] Such normative orders are capable of truly exercising legitimate power, of being authoritative, where there is a clear connection to the individual's autonomy. This then gives rise to the question of whether the nature of binding rules external to the person ever truly exists: is authority something of a mirage, in that individuals exercise autonomy in complying or not? Wolff makes this argument in a compelling fashion, particularly from the perspective of a participant in a Western liberal democratic system. He argues that everyone has the right to disobey the law and, in fact, a more realistic approach is to acknowledge that legitimate authority cannot exist because this would undermine complete autonomy.[44] The acceptance of systems of rules and other traditions speaks, in his view, to a degree of moral apathy and he argues that there is no moral command to obey the State.[45] However, this does not really work in the context of criminal law. The moral dimension to criminal law means that there is a degree of overlap between morality and law: those who do not murder avoid doing so because of both legal constraints and moral aversion. The idea that lawmakers would be issuing the sole command not to murder is not supported by even a brief consideration of the issue. Indeed, Shapiro develops this argument by noting that it would be morally irresponsible to cede too much decision-making to others, and that authorities claim immense power beyond that which

38 ibid 96.

39 ibid 102–103.

40 Nicole Roughan, *Authorities: Conflicts, Cooperation and Transnational Legal Theories* (Oxford University Press 2013), 32.

41 Raz, *Authority* (n 7) 12.

42 Samantha Besson, 'State Consent and Disagreement in International Law-Making: Dissolving the Paradox' (2016) 29 LJIL 289, 302.

43 ibid.

44 Wolff (n 21) 22–24.

45 ibid 30.

they possess.[46] As such, lawmakers may issue certain instructions with which compliance has already been guaranteed through personal adherence to other values. The engagement of the individual's autonomy may grant authority to the act, but the role of autonomy exerts greater influence over the outcome of compliance than the exercise of power by the lawmaker. Accordingly, an understanding of autonomy is necessary to understand authority.

2.3 THE QUESTION OF AUTONOMY

Shapiro's argument that it would be morally irresponsible to allow others to make too many decisions for us[47] is intriguing; it highlights the direct bearing that autonomy has on authority. There may well be an individual responsibility for moral decision-making which continues to rest with the individual regardless of the power that authorities claim because of the individual responsibility that everyone has for their own moral decisions. To examine this idea further, Wolff's idea of complete autonomy mandating anarchy should be examined.

The idea of autonomy is critical to that of the justification of authority set out by Raz, and that which justifies the exercise of power at the domestic level. And yet, with full autonomy would arrive anarchy, as argued by Wolff.[48] It is a strong argument, based on the conception of autonomy rooted in a Kantian approach to responsibility: autonomy is an amalgam of freedom and responsibility. As individuals must make moral decisions in respect of their own lives, they are autonomous[49] and directly responsible for the choices they make. Personal autonomy in the view of Raz is similar, although with fewer moral overtones: the autonomous individual is the 'part author of his life' and may make decisions freely.[50] The inclusion of 'part' in the definition acknowledges that autonomy is naturally limited by competing interests, meaning that there has to be some sort of limitation on personal autonomy if people are to live among one another in a degree of harmony. This is particularly important where there are plural systems of authority with which individuals will seek to comply, including external systems of morality. May cites religion as an

46 Scott Shapiro, 'Authority' 382–439 in Jules Coleman and Scott Shapiro (eds), *The Oxford Handbook of Jurisprudence and the Philosophy of Law* (Oxford University Press 2002), 383 and 388.

47 ibid.

48 Wolff (n 21) 24.

49 ibid 22–24.

50 Joseph Raz, *The Morality of Freedom* (Oxford University Press 1986), 370.

example which influences individual autonomy[51] and uses Aristotle's work to support the idea that autonomy is critical for personal responsibility.[52] May agrees that autonomy should be exercised when complying with the law, secondary to the law's authority.[53] This idea of personal responsibility for individual decision-making in relation to compliance with the law or morality in general is cogent: individuals can, very clearly, choose not to obey the law or to follow certain social rules. Wolff notes that the exercise of autonomy would directly conflict with the acceptance of authority if all reasons for action were considered equally important.[54] Should there be other, valid reasons for action, we could perhaps engage autonomy by considering them and then obeying. However, this is not considered, as the whole idea is absolute: either authority or autonomy exists, but not both. May identifies that some authority may be legitimate when grounds for justification can be found to allow individuals to act in line with authority, in situations where it falls in line with their autonomy.

Raz, however, sets out conditions for the legitimacy of authority by justifying the exercise of a right to rule through direct engagement with autonomy.[55] Rather than examining the position of the sovereign as the basis on which an individual might accept rules, his concept looks at the reasons for obedience that an individual might have. In this way, he reconciles Wolff's idea that complete autonomy would require complete anarchy and acknowledges that individuals will seek to comply when there are reasons which adequately support that compliance. This problem of non-conforming, which would then undermine both the rule and the system and their existence[56] can thus be ameliorated. Moreover, such compliance in line with such reasons would be legitimate. This thesis is particularly important for autonomy and authority, as authority's distinction from power is dependent on it being a legitimate exercise of power. Without these carefully considered elements, the exercise of power would remain as such, without authority. It would then be difficult to justify authority as legitimate without recourse to individual autonomy. The limitations which authority places on autonomy should also be recognised to avoid the conception that anarchy is necessary, as fully autonomous decision-making is possible in a society without anarchy, on the basis that the law can be broken. Autonomy does not require unrestricted liberty because, as noted above,

51 Thomas May, *Autonomy, Authority and Moral Responsibility* (Springer 1998), 4.
52 ibid 38.
53 ibid 122.
54 Raz, *The Authority of Law* (n 1) 27.
55 Raz, *The Morality of Freedom* (n 50) 23.
56 Raz, *The Authority of Law* (n 1) 87.

individuals may comply with the law and generate authority through the exercise of their autonomy. Autonomy does not guarantee anarchy, at all.[57]

The thesis set out by Raz to engage the concepts of authority and autonomy is known as the normal justification thesis. It can be summarised as what he considers to be the typical approach to authority: one complies because one is better off doing so than not.[58] More specifically, the reasons for which one complies are more likely to be met if the directives of the authority are considered binding and followed as such.[59] Issuing directives in such a way would comply with the idea of authority as a legitimate exercise of power: one exercises the power which individuals both recognise and with which they seek to comply because it supports their reasons for acting in the first place. Acknowledging that there are many reasons for which individuals act, this concept of both autonomy and authority recognises the plural demands on those who have the freedom to act, noting that compliance with the law is rarely the primary justification for action. This balance of reasons[60] which are considered by the individual is then part of why the law may be a legitimate exercise of power, where compliance rests principally with the individual and not the lawmaker.

This approach would undermine arguments regarding the passing of authority and autonomy to others, including democratic representatives for the purpose of creating rules.[61] Autonomy is not franchised or licensed to others under a democratic system, but instead is exercised frequently and in a multiplicity of contexts. It also accounts for why rules are broken, and why certain rules, such as parking stipulations, might be broken more frequently than others. The individual acting autonomously acts for a variety of reasons, and the authority of the lawmaker, as stated earlier, would rarely be considered as a principal reason for action. In line with this argument, authority can be regarded as advice that one cannot ignore: there is no force, no coercion, only the notion that one acts in a certain way because it is good, right, and the way that things should be done.[62] In generating internal compliance, because the individual wishes to comply for reasons connected to their intrinsic

57 Although not legal theory, the idea that people are not prone to self-interested anarchy is worked through in detail using historical examples in Rutger Bregman, *Humankind: A Hopeful History* (Bloomsbury 2020).

58 Raz, *The Morality of Freedom* (n 50) 23.

59 ibid 53.

60 May (n 51).

61 David B Goldman, *Globalisation and the Western Legal Tradition: Recurring Patterns of Law and Authority* (Cambridge University Press 2007), 301.

62 Arendt (n 2) 123.

motivations, the link between legitimacy and power, as authority, is much clearer. Legitimacy is a characteristic of certain exercises of power and gives such exercises their authority.

Thus, autonomy is a key aspect of authority as a legitimate exercise of power. Raz notes that law as an exercise of power demonstrates the link between authority and power, but this allows a distinction between the two which offers a justification for the exercise of power. For an exercise of power to be considered legitimate, it must engage with the autonomy of the individual, otherwise the justifications for such exercises of power detach from explanations of how authority works in democratic societies. This element of autonomy is critical because it acknowledges that individuals do not need to obey the law and may also obey rules which stem from sources of authority beyond the law itself. Raz notes that this is part of why the law may possess legitimacy: it does not compel or threaten, and indeed is broken in many situations. He highlights the legitimacy which underlies authority specifically, and further separates the obligation to obey the law for moral reasons and because of the law's legitimate claim to power.[63] Thus, law possesses legitimacy, and thereby authority, where it can demonstrate that it constitutes a legitimate exercise of power. It does so where individuals are following the law wherever it conforms to reason to do so,[64] and where individuals can recognise that the directives are authoritative because they comply with certain intrinsic motivations as well. His focus on the reasons for action form the basis of his account of authority.

The next question, then, is what is meant by legitimacy. Based on the above conception, authority which considers the autonomy of the individual would be sufficiently legitimate. However, this does not consider fully what is meant by legitimacy, or how these ideas could impact on criminal law. Indeed, the questions above regarding the authority of law and its considered legitimacy are particularly contentious in criminal law, because of the way in which criminal law directly regulates behaviour. In areas such as contract law, principles such as consent and capacity, a willingness to agree and an ability to understand that by which you agree to be bound, are key to the enforcement of contractual provisions. There is no such engagement in criminal law with the notion of consent, and therefore it naturally limits autonomy. The next part to the discussion considers legitimacy before turning to the issue of how authority, legitimacy, autonomy, and the criminal law interact.

63 Raz, *The Authority of Law* (n 1) 236.

64 Joseph Raz, *Between Authority and Interpretation: On the Theory of Law and Practical Reason* (Oxford University Press 2009), 137.

2.4 THE CONCEPT OF LEGITIMACY

The definition of legitimacy links to lawfulness, which is not particularly helpful when discussing the law or when trying to understand its underlying authority. Legitimacy can also be discussed as a condition precedent for the existence of authority,[65] or referred to as an issue, particularly for international courts and institutions.[66] There are few explicit discussions of the concept of legitimacy and what it might mean, particularly when discussing authority, power, and autonomy. This exploration therefore attempts to understand what is meant by legitimacy and what makes the law legitimate, as well as how it links to power.

Raz makes two points regarding his perspective on what legitimacy may be: he identifies its origin as in the moral bedrock of such institutions[67] and that such legitimacy is rooted in their ability to achieve 'desirable social coordination.'[68] Similarly to authority, legitimacy cannot simply be that one possesses the power, but rather that there is an underlying reason for both possessing and exercising the power. This links it to authority, in the view of Raz, which is a justification right without obligation.[69] The foregoing understanding of authority, considering the idea of autonomy, is that judgment ought to be surrendered to the authority as the most rational course of action.[70] The rational act does not create the legitimacy, but it is rather a desirable condition, a reason for acting. The exercise of power is thus justified by it being rational to surrender to the authority, exercising one's autonomy and thereby creating sufficient conditions to recognise the legitimacy of the decision or institution. Here, Raz acknowledges a link between authority and power because of the legitimacy which underlies authority specifically.[71] As noted by Hannah Arendt, although both force and authority can compel people to obey; only one method has legitimacy in doing so.[72] The use of force is

65 Weber (n 5) 1–11.

66 See, for example, Daniel Bodansky, 'The Concept of Legitimacy in International Law' 309–317 in Rudiger Wolfrum and Volker Roben (eds), *Legitimacy in International Law* (Springer 2008); Allen Buchanan, 'The Legitimacy of International Law' 79 in John Tasioulas and Samantha Besson (eds), *The Philosophy of International Law* (Oxford University Press 2010).

67 Raz, *Between Authority and Interpretation* (n 64) 188.

68 Raz, *Authority* (n 7) 14.

69 Joseph Raz, 'Authority and Justification' 115–141 in Joseph Raz (ed), *Authority* (Basil Blackwell 1990), 116.

70 ibid 139.

71 Raz, *The Authority of Law* (n 1) 236.

72 Arendt (n 2) 102–103.

something which is possible via the exercise of power, but the accordant acts would lack legitimacy if all force were used to guarantee obedience. Arendt adroitly sets out the necessity of legitimacy for the authoritative exercise of power without going into too much detail of what this might mean, or how it might be identified. This is a common issue in the literature, where legitimacy is identified as necessary without explaining what it might mean.

As noted earlier, there are few studies of legitimacy which do not refer to authority or, indeed, which conflate the concepts of authority and legitimacy. Weber's work on legitimate authority[73] appears to view one as part of the other and vice versa, while critiques of his work tend to focus entirely on the discussion as a conception of legitimacy.[74] Work on international law focuses to a far greater extent on the idea of legitimacy, which will be discussed as part of the next chapter, perhaps because of the problems associated with the authority and legitimacy of international law. The idea of political legitimacy at the domestic level is thus often connected directly to authority, and there appear to be few attempts to separate the two. For Weber, legitimacy is connected directly to the authority of the political system: the existence of legal authority is connected to the administrative and judicial nature of the principles underpinning the rules. The rule of law, effectively, is that which limits power and accords the authority in question their legitimacy.[75] Raz concurs with the idea that untrammelled authority can never be legitimate,[76] indicating the separateness of the two concepts. He discusses, unsurprisingly, the two ideas to the greatest extent of any political or legal philosopher, although most agree on the idea of legitimacy as the justification, or attempted justification, of the exercise of power.[77] Thus, legitimacy appears to limit power when exercised, and could perhaps relate to the existence of certain institutions or their formation. Legitimacy is thus the justified exercise of power for specific reasons, and, when viewed through the lens of Raz's theories on authority, is when the institution or decision permits the exercise of autonomy when it acts with the power it already possesses.

The idea of legitimacy may be a feature of the exercise of power: power can either be legitimately exercised or not. In the latter case, the exercise of power would be founded on oppression. Arguably, all exercises of power are coercive

[73] Weber (n 5) 1.

[74] Peter Stillmann, 'A Concept of Legitimacy' (1974) 7 Polity 32; RW Smith, 'The Concept of Legitimacy' (1970) 35 Theoria 17.

[75] Weber (n 5) 1–11.

[76] Raz, *Authority* (n 7) 12.

[77] Raz, *The Authority of Law* (n 1) 27; Lawrence Friedman, *The Republic of Choice: Law, Authority and Culture* (Harvard University Press 1990), 39 and 211.

to an extent. In the view of Nagel, political legitimacy is the history of attempts to discover a way of justifying coercively imposed political and social institutions to the people who must live under them.[78] Thus the element of coercion is an intrinsic part of the exercise of power, even where it is authoritative. This connects well to Wolff's idea that much in society is accepted which should not be, such as monarchic rule through which power passes from one generation of a family to the next.[79] This creates significant problems for democratic societies because the argument here is that any coercive laws or decisions would undermine the legitimacy of the exercise of power, draining it of any authority. It would appear then that areas such as criminal law would qualify as such, without some engagement with the autonomy of individuals. Reconciling the two is difficult, but possible. This acceptance of, effectively, illegitimate means of decision-making or exercises of powers undermines the legitimacy of the law because there is no engagement by the people in the decision to create or continue these institutions. The idea underlying the legitimacy of the rules is that there should be full acceptance by the community in a way which mandates engagement.

There must therefore be something beyond individual autonomy on a purely individual basis to justify the use of power as legitimate. Certain rules also are followed by more than one individual acting autonomously, particularly those in criminal law. The legal prohibition on murder, as discussed earlier, is a good example of a rule which is followed by individuals who are guided by their autonomy as well as the law, in both a collective and individual sense. Legal rules demonstrate their legitimacy through their standing in individual political communities:[80] the community agrees on a certain standard and therefore it is enforced by law.[81] Standards both bind and belong to the community.[82] This indicates that consent has occurred somewhere, either through democratic processes or via the representation of the will of the people. The criminal law, in respect of crimes against the person, demonstrates some elements of this legitimacy, but not all. Communities and groupings of individuals accept certain aspects of the criminal law, such as the prohibition on murder, for reasons that relate to both their autonomy and the legitimacy of the prohibition. The rule is legitimate because of both its

78 Thomas Nagel, 'Moral Conflict and Political Legitimacy' 300–324, in Joseph Raz (ed), *Authority* (Basil Blackwell 1990), 302.

79 Wolff (n 21) 22–24.

80 Raz, *Between Authority and Interpretation* (n 64), 101.

81 ibid 102.

82 ibid.

support and the guidance it provides to society, despite the way in which it limits autonomy through the restraint on certain acts.

The next section looks at this idea in greater detail, by exploring the link between legitimacy, autonomy, authority, and the criminal law. From the discussion above, it has been demonstrated acts will have authority where the actor or institution exercises power in a legitimate fashion. Both its authority and legitimacy are innately linked to the autonomy of the individual, alone and as part of a community. A question arises, however, with the area of criminal law, which directly restrains individual autonomy through proscribing certain acts. Although, as discussed earlier, most individuals do adhere to the criminal law because of other reasons, the connection between autonomy, legitimacy, and the criminal law needs to be further evidenced. Should legitimacy and the law's authority rest on the engagement with autonomy, an area such as criminal law which proscribes and punishes behaviour presents a unique challenge to the theory. A more detailed discussion is therefore required.

2.5 THE LINK BETWEEN AUTHORITY, LEGITIMACY, AND CRIMINAL LAW

The questions of legitimacy and authority in relation to criminal law are gravely understudied; there is a significant gap in the law literature in this area. One of the few pieces, and one which was published recently, was authored by Bennett[83] and examined the legitimacy of the criminal law. This is a fascinating gap, particularly because of the way in which the legitimacy of criminal law beyond the State has been studied extensively,[84] creating a body of scholarship in specific areas of transnational and international criminal law. Although it is not clear as to why there is such little discussion, particularly when the question of legitimacy is so critical for international law, it is accepted that there can be a difficulty in applying the ideas explored earlier to the concept of criminal law. Where authority is considered a legitimate exercise of power, and it must engage with personal

[83] Christopher Bennett, 'The Authority of Moral Oversight: On the Legitimacy of Criminal Law' (2019) 25 LT 153–177.

[84] Eleanor Spaventa, 'Opening Pandora's Box: Some Reflections on the Constitutional Effects of the Decision in Pupino' (2007) 3 ECLR 5; Irene Wieczorek, *The Legitimacy of EU Criminal Law* (Hart 2020); Nobuo Hayashi and Cecilia M Bailliet (eds), *The Legitimacy of International Criminal Tribunals* (Cambridge University Press 2017); Allen Buchanan, 'The Legitimacy of International Law,' and David Luban, 'Fairness to Rights: Jurisdiction, Legality and the Legitimacy of International Criminal Law,' both in John Tasioulas and Samantha Besson (eds), *The Philosophy of International Law* (Oxford University Press 2010).

autonomy to be considered legitimate, then how may this apply to criminal law? Domestic criminal law tends to lack the engagement, similarly, with the concept of autonomy in this context, as discussed earlier: it is unquestionably an exercise of power, but it does directly restrict individual autonomy.

Although criminal law entails moral responsibility, via the duty not to murder, abuse, or steal, it also engages with regulation which does not necessarily deal with a moral issue. Tax evasion is a notable example. There is nothing to say that every aspect of the criminal law engages with moral responsibility for the individual. Instead, it places limits on behaviour. Moreover, those areas which do deal with moral responsibility, primarily crimes against the person, require criminal law to bind individuals without regard for their autonomy. The criminal law does not necessarily look to morality for guidance on how to deal with crimes against the person. Indeed, criminal law proscribes certain conduct without engaging in a discussion of whether one agrees with the ideas. Those who are unwilling to restrict their autonomy in the area of criminal conduct are likely to be prosecuted. If law requires engagement with autonomy in order to legitimately exercise power, and thus possess authority, how can criminal law have authority without engaging with individual autonomy? Does it automatically lack legitimacy because of its failure to afford individuals appropriate autonomy? A simplistic, perhaps absurdist, answer would be that it does indeed lack legitimacy: it is not a legitimate use of power because it does not allow all individuals, as individuals, to consent to the rules and to agree to follow them. However, this would be quite a facetious approach to undertake: the corollary to this argument is that the prohibition on murder lacks legitimacy because individuals who wish to murder are not able to exercise their autonomy in line with their wishes, nor do they accept the limitations placed on their behaviour by the State. The focus on restricting autonomy by criminal law, in a manner conforming to the legitimate exercise of power, is that legitimacy must also mean something more than simply a legitimate exercise of power. It must, in some way, go beyond the requirement to engage with individual autonomy. Indeed, there must be a facet to authority, and thereby legitimacy, which considers other ideas relevant to the social aims of criminal law, and the enhancement of society overall.

Part of the purpose of a criminal law system is to ensure that justice is done, and that individuals are protected from significant harm at the hands of another. The balance between the freedom to act as one wishes, in complete autonomy, and the right of another to live without violence being done to them is one which must be acknowledged and supported by the legal system. This can be seen in areas such as human rights law, where there must be a balance between the exercise of rights by individuals and the way in which it affects the rights and freedoms of others. The failure to acknowledge the rights and freedoms of others prevents the exercise of the initial right and, moreover, may affect their legitimacy. One cannot exercise power or a prerogative where it affects another's freedom directly; there must be a balance between one's right to act and another individual's right to live without harm being done. The corollary to this argument is that criminal law should not over-regulate, and unduly restrict behaviour, but instead focuses on prevention of harm. It could be argued, in another time and place, that any criminal law which does not seek to prevent harm may lack legitimacy, but that which protects individuals, particularly in the context of the rights and freedoms of others, may successfully be held as a legitimate exercise of power.

That which connects authority, legitimacy, and criminal law can thus be observed. Authority as a legitimate exercise of power creates the link between authority and legitimacy and requires that all exercises of power be legitimate to accept the rule or decision as legitimate and therefore authoritative. The legitimacy of the rule is predicated on the acceptance of the rule as a good reason, through the exercise of personal autonomy. In the case of criminal law, the role of autonomy is less significant than the protection of individuals from harm, and the greater focus on the protection of individual rights and freedoms, which may otherwise be undermined by individuals who seek to cause harm.

Authority and legitimacy are deeply connected; one emerges as a condition for the other in that power must be exercised legitimately to possess the requisite authority. Law must possess this authority to be followed; it must demonstrate the link between the behaviour and influence on that behaviour to be accepted by the actors. This is particularly critical in the case of criminal law, as criminal law has a significant role to play in ensuring justice and protecting individuals in society. At the same time, it restricts the behaviour of the individual to such an extent that the power underlying it must be justified with reference to something beyond an understanding that those who make the law are entitled to do so. If the issue cannot be linked to autonomy, it must be accepted that there is either no authority for the exercise of power in respect of criminal law, or a different basis. The different basis, which makes greater sense than the reliance on autonomy, is on the idea of criminal law as justice, as a means of protection. That idea is critical for the functioning of a society, to ensure that the vulnerable are adequately protected and supported, and to ensure that the idea of autonomy is not warped by those who would seek to abuse others in the name of freedom.

Consequently, the authority possessed by criminal law, specifically in relation to crimes against the person, can be traced to the function of the law as providing justice. Its authority does not support autonomy, but rather the functioning of a society in which we would wish to live. This protection focuses on the prevention of harm, rather than the support for untrammelled autonomy. Rather than supporting an underlying morality, it protects those who would be exploited and restrains damaging, harmful behaviour. As an exercise of power, it is legitimate where it ensures justice for those who would otherwise be exploited and abused. The limits of this understanding lie in areas which do not concern crimes against the person: it is difficult to argue that the law criminalising certain traffic violations is legitimate to ensure justice and the protection of the vulnerable. However, it could be linked to a situation in which individuals may be harmed: driving through a red light is not inherently bad, but where there is a pedestrian crossing, a failure to stop may result in the death of a pedestrian. Consequently, the protective function of the criminal law may be reflected even in provisions which are not directly connected to crimes against the person, but where harm to an individual is likely to be done without the existence of a rule to at least deter the commission of that harm. Thus, it is possible for criminal law to be justified as legitimate, and therefore authoritative, in that the aim of preventing harm may justify limiting personal autonomy.

The difficulty in asserting a complete theory of criminal law is demonstrated earlier; criminal law, more so than other areas of law, exercises power in the most significant way over individual autonomy; it prescribes how one must behave within society and the harms that one is not bound to do. Criminal law is not a form of morality but rather a threshold of behaviour acceptable to society, below which one must not descend without encountering consequences.

This makes it impossible for it to engage with individual autonomy completely, because it places direct restrictions on individual behaviour, albeit desirable restrictions to which most people do not object. It cannot be characterised, consequently, as a form of advice that you must follow, as most individuals would not wish to cause harm to another individual. Rather the conclusion reached here is that the authority of criminal law, as a legitimate exercise of State power, connects to its ability to achieve justice and maintain fairness, particularly for vulnerable individuals. Its focus is less on the ability to encourage and advise, and more to protect from harm. Thus, its authority stems from its protective function, its ability to provide justice where breaches occur. Criminal law cannot achieve legitimacy, or claim to be authoritative, without fulfilling that function. This conclusion equally avoids the problems created by a purely moral reading of the criminal law, which rely on a moral universalism to justify the proscription of certain crimes. Rather than engaging in a relativist or universalist reading, the protection from harm is both a useful understanding of the law and one which offers intellectual coherence to an area which does not subscribe to the conceptualisations outlined above of authority and legitimacy.

2.6 CONCLUSION

The arguments made here demonstrate the link between authority and legitimacy, and the way in which authority has been shown as necessary if exercises of power are to be legitimate. The concept of authority at the domestic level has been extensively debated, with a focus on the ability to determine the rules that others will follow. Earlier conceptions of authority rested on the provision of a command, while more recent approaches, focusing on liberal, democratic societies, engage with the idea of personal autonomy. An understanding of authority is critical for exercises of power in societies which profess the importance of freedom to their constitution, and the concept of autonomy is thus key to understanding authority. Similarly, legitimacy is a critical part of authority: the legitimate exercise of power confers authority on the law and allows the acts committed under the authority of the law to be considered legitimate. Rather than looking at legitimacy as a form of lawfulness, it should be viewed as the basis for authority: legitimate exercises of power will possess authority. However, legitimacy also engages with the idea of autonomy, requiring legitimate exercises of power to consider the autonomy of the individual. The link between authority and legitimacy is clear: legitimacy is a condition which must be met in respect of any exercise of power in order to be considered authoritative. The authority of rules, and law more generally, cannot exist unless legitimacy underpins the exercise of that power. This underscores the importance of autonomy: rules cannot be imposed on individuals in a free society without some engagement with them, and individuals should be free to act and to behave in society as they wish. The tension which exists, however, in such situations, is between this and the question of proscription under criminal law.

While these conceptions of authority and legitimacy are useful for the purposes of law and political authority in general, where the individual follows the rule as a form of 'good advice' or is persuaded of the value of the law, the criterion of autonomy is problematic in relation to criminal law. This is chiefly because of the restrictions it places on autonomy. The requirement that an individual may exercise autonomy is useful, generally, in a free society as it recognises the rights of the individual and provides a response to the exercise of State power. However, in respect of criminal law, there are general and valid restrictions on autonomy. There are, indeed, very good reasons for restricting individual behaviour where that behaviour is likely to harm others. As such, criminal law can be justified as legitimate where the aim is prevention of harm and provision of justice, and it may limit autonomy insofar as it achieves this aim.

The necessity of authority for criminal law is particularly important, as law which restricts and moderates behaviour must be authoritative for it to be followed. As there is no way of relying fully on personal autonomy, its legitimacy must be justified in another way. The legitimacy of criminal law thus relies on the way in which it balances the rights and freedoms of different members of society to achieve its authority. It is a method of justice, as such, a means of preventing the injury and misery that would otherwise arise if there was an untrammelled ability for individuals to act without consequence. At the international level, it is difficult to translate this directly: States have much more freedom than individuals, and some have far more power. There is much greater autonomy in such cases, which then creates an issue for authority. The next chapter will explore the idea of authority at the international level, identifying how international law may have authority and how the different approaches to authority at the international level impact on its ability to exercise power in a legitimate fashion.

3

The Authority of Public International Law

3.1 INTRODUCTION

As mentioned in Chapter 2, there is a greater discussion of authority and legitimacy, in general, in the context of international law, and public international law in particular. That discussion focused on the connection between authority and legitimacy at the domestic level, concluding that the authority of law is the legitimate exercise of power. Moreover, domestic governments can justify the authority of their acts, and laws specifically, where they engage with individual autonomy. This is particularly significant in areas such as criminal law, which does not seek to engage with individual reason but instead creates prohibitions by which everyone must abide regardless of their individual autonomy. Although individual compliance with criminal law is usually expected, the imposition of criminal sanctions and the wider prevention of harm, as well as the provision of justice, are equally significant considerations. Limiting human behaviour in this way, limiting individual autonomy, is a public good which does not undermine the legitimacy or authority of criminal law.

However, even criminal law, and domestic law in general, has an advantage over public international law when analysing its authority. The acts of the State, or sovereign, at the domestic level, can be analysed and the laws made considered in light of the concepts of autonomy, legitimacy, and authority, and the way in which these impact upon individuals. When States make law with other States, what gives them that authority? The concept of autonomy can seem very distant from ordinary individuals in society, despite many areas of public international law binding them and affecting their lives. The idea of international law-making as a legitimate exercise of power can seem arbitrary. As such, this chapter examines the extent to which public international law has authority, whether the understanding of authority posited thus far could ever apply to the international system, or whether the legitimate exercise of power is conceptualised in an entirely different way in public international law.

There has been some discussion, historically, on the source of international law's authority, distinct from that of domestic legal theory. Grotius noted that the State's authority and right to govern was based on the collective agreement of the citizenry[1] which, when applied to public international law, would mean that international law derives its authority from a collective of States. However, Grotius did not expand upon this point and so the conclusion here remains that international law has authority because States have authority, without any justification or exploration offered. Vitoria instead focuses on the idea that all individuals have reason and that this natural law, the natural order, must be respected by others, particularly where the 'State' or grouping of individuals is organised under a system.[2] Again, the focus is on the authority of States as they are, although a slightly greater degree of exposition, rooted in reason, is offered.

Vitoria's main contribution was to undermine the universality of papal authority, revising the idea of authority in line with natural law, but his work did not fully conclude as to why public international law ought to have authority: the account of why reason would give States authority at the international level would need to have been discussed in greater detail. It was not considered that reason might not guide the individuals who run States, nor that the approach to reasoning may vary in different States, motivated by different concerns. Although Grotius and Vitoria explore authority to a different extent, both were natural lawyers, focusing on a reasoned, rational account of how international law is made and operates. For modern public international law, the natural law approach has given way to positivism, as evidenced by Hall.[3] In his work, he notes that the idea of natural law in international law collapsed during the Enlightenment, but also that positivism is too meagre a basis on which to understand public international law. Indeed, its acceptance as an understanding of public international law is detrimental to certain areas, such as human rights law because it does not permit, for example, an understanding of the idea of justice. An overly positivist approach would disregard other concepts as part of the system and ignore the role that concepts such as justice and human rights play in the international legal system.

1 Hugo Grotius, *Commentary on the Law of Prize and Booty* (Oxford University Press 1950).

2 Francisco de Vitoria (ed AR Pagden and Jeremy Lawrance), *Vitoria: Political Writings* (Cambridge University Press 1991).

3 Stephen Hall, 'The Persistent Spectre: Natural Law, International Order and the Limits of Positivism' (2001) 12 EJIL 269.

More recent legal theory works have focused squarely on the problem: Kelsen's theories were applied to public international law by von Bernstorff.[4] Çali[5] equally discusses the idea of consent as the source of the authority of international law, dealing with the idea that the authority of international law has a direct relationship with the authority of domestic law. There have been other texts written on the idea of the importance of the State: Criddle and Fox-Decent[6] argue for a system which relies on States as the guardians of rights, while Teitel[7] focuses on an order outwith statehood that restrains State action and protects rights in international law. Besson similarly focuses on the autonomy of the individual as the source of international law's authority.[8] Franck's seminal text on legitimacy[9] supports the idea that States obey the law when it is legitimate, and therefore that the law possesses greater authority when legitimate, leading to a circular proof which does not offer much in the way of an answer to the questions posed here. The recent work carried out by Alter, Helfer, and Madsen focuses on a context-dependent theory of authority.[10] In the context of international criminal law, this would mean that its authority is dependent on the actor to whom it is directed. This may then, through the lens of the theory of Alter, Helfer, and Madsen, be a 'narrow' form of authority because of the reluctance of those to whom it is directed to take it seriously as a form of law. This is a prior question to that of compliance, instead focusing on whether the individuals concerned consider the law to be 'law' and recognise it as such.

The question of the authority of public international law thus requires an examination of authority beyond the positivist–natural law dichotomy, undertaking a fresh analysis of the problem. This chapter will thus examine whether the authority of international law is rooted in State consent, as a legitimate exercise of State power. The legitimate nature of that exercise of power, and how legitimacy might be conferred on States will then be discussed. The role

4 Jochen von Bernstorff, *The Public International Law Theory of Hans Kelsen: Believing in Universal Law* (Cambridge University Press 2010).

5 Başak Çali, *The Authority of International Law: Obedience, Respect and Rebuttal* (Oxford University Press 2015).

6 Evan J Criddle and Ewan Fox-Decent, *Fiduciaries of Humanity: How International Law Constitutes Authority* (Oxford University Press 2016).

7 Ruti Teitel, *Humanity's Law* (Oxford University Press 2011).

8 Samantha Besson, 'The Authority of International Law – Lifting the State Veil' (2009) 31 Sydney LR 343.

9 Thomas Franck, *The Power of Legitimacy among Nations* (Oxford University Press 1990).

10 Mikael Madsen, Karen Alter and Lawrence Helfer, *International Court Authority* (Oxford University Press 2018).

played by morality, as an external force or guiding principle of international law, will then be explored to conclude the arguments made in the chapter.

3.2 IS CONSENT THE ROOT OF AUTHORITY IN INTERNATIONAL LAW?

The authority of international law, if it relates only to the States themselves, could be argued to be State consent. It is a basic principle of public international law that States give their willing agreement to be bound by rules created by them through consensus. If States possess the authority to make law at the domestic level, surely that authority would then simply transfer to the international level? Clearly, States possess power at the international level, to make and break rules, and to raise actions against other States. Through the creation and recognition of rules, they possess what Joseph Raz refers to as 'power to require action.'[11] Arguably this would be tantamount to authority, since even at the domestic level Razian authority is a 'species of power,'[12] and, specifically, this would entail the power to affect reasons for compliance. This domestic authority could relate to the power exercised at the international level, thus perhaps transferring to the international level, to justify the creation of rules. However, there is no guarantee that such power would be exercised legitimately and thereby could claim authority. The exercise of that power would need to be examined, to determine whether the acts the State undertakes are authoritative. When the State is acting at the international level, it may have power without authority unless the exercise of power can be evidenced as legitimate. The process of making international rules, through consent and consensus, may direct the inquiry a little further, as States must consent to being bound by the rule. The consent of legitimate governments, as well as the requirement that other States consent, could justify the exercise of power as legitimate.

However, Raz holds that it may be in the interests of the State to consent,[13] but it is not the consent itself which creates the authority of the law. Indeed, the exercise of consent, as an exercise of power, would need to be examined in order to appreciate whether it was a legitimate exercise of State power. Developing this idea further, I would argue that consenting to the creation of a rule is an exercise of power: it demonstrates the ability of the State to

[11] Joseph Raz, *The Morality of Freedom* (Oxford University Press 1988), 38.
[12] Joseph Raz, *The Authority of Law* (1st edn, Oxford University Press 1979), 18.
[13] Raz, *The Morality of Freedom* (n 11) 80.

create law through its actions but does not necessarily evidence the legitimacy of the exercise of that power.

Libya, for example, ratified several human rights treaties during the reign of Colonel Gaddafi.[14] However, the amendment to the Libyan Constitution he appended[15] cites a system of direct democracy as the authority of the exercise of power. However, the people had never elected him, as he had seized power, and there was no system of constitutional checks and balances by which his power could be limited. The government he created under the amendment, with a series of congresses and committees, did not have any explicit constitutional basis or explanation of their power. The book he wrote setting out his ideas rejects the constitutional basis of power and cites 'tradition or religion' instead as the basis for the authority of law.[16] On this basis, as well as the method by which he acquired power, there is little to demonstrate that Libya had the domestic authority to create rules and any authority at the international level. Gaddafi's power was unquestionably visible; his authority was not. The consent of the Libyan government, such as it was, did not adequately demonstrate its authority at either the domestic or international level.

This demonstrates the conceptualisation of consent as an exercise of power, underscoring how critical this is, given the central position of the State in international law and the requirement that States consent to any laws being made. As public international law is regarded primarily as a 'decision-making process,'[17] and the positivist view of international law is that agreement is required to make the law,[18] then the consent of States is a central element of the law-making process. This is what Koskenneimi refers to as the 'political character'[19] of law-making at the international level, in that the political power of States allows them to consent. This is not to say that there is a great deal of focus on the power States exercise at the international level when making

[14] The International Covenant on Economic, Social and Cultural Rights (ICESCR), ratified by Libya in 1976; The International Covenant on Civil and Political Rights (ICCPR), ratified by Libya in 1976; The Convention on the Elimination of All Forms of Discrimination against Women (CEDAW), ratified by Libya in 1989; The Convention against Torture and Other Cruel, Inhuman or Degrading Treatment or Punishment (CAT), ratified by Libya in 1989. See 'Libya: Words to Deeds, The Urgent Need for Human Rights Reform' (2006) 18 Human Rights Watch 1E.

[15] *Libya: Declaration on the Establishment of the Authority of the People*, 2 March 1977.

[16] Muammar al-Qaddafi, *Green Book* (Medina University Press 2021), 27.

[17] Rosalyn Higgins, 'Thinking about the Individual in International Law' (1978) 4 BJIS 1, 5 and Jean D'Aspremont, *Formalism and the Sources of International Law: A Theory of the Ascertainment of Legal Rules* (Oxford University Press 2011), 106.

[18] Michael Byers, *Custom, Power and the Power of Rules* (Cambridge University Press 1999), 9.

[19] Martti Koskenniemi, *From Apology to Utopia* (Cambridge University Press 2006), 387.

rules: Byers laments the ignorance of the role power has in international law-making, particularly custom,[20] in that consent is rarely regarded as an exercise of power. It is difficult to conclude that consent is the root of authority if it is just an exercise of power, without investigating its legitimacy somewhat. Moreover, acquiescence may contribute to the formation of legal norms,[21] meaning that consent is not required in every situation. In such cases, would the acts or laws lack authority because there has been no exercise of power? Or would such situations lack legitimacy?

Such an understanding requires an examination of the basis on which States consent. Primarily, States which may consent to legal norms, and be bound by such rules, are those which possess the characteristics of Statehood and are recognised by the international community as such.[22] The sovereignty of such States would be recognised, and they could exercise power as a consequence of their sovereignty, by engaging with the international system, through rule creation and entering into treaties with other States. That is not to say that consent in terms of ratifying treaties alone is sufficient to demonstrate the authority of States,[23] as the mere ability to consent, the exercise of power, is not sufficient to evidence their legitimacy in doing so. However, the sovereignty of States provides a useful point of departure to understand why or whether such consent might be legitimate.

The ability to exercise power at the international level, and potentially the ability to meet the criteria for statehood, depends on the ability of a State to govern itself. This would typically be evidenced through the existence of a constitutional system under which the State operates. Accordingly, sovereign nations which base the ability to consent on domestic constitutional norms have potential authority which could be demonstrated through the exercise of their consent at the international level. The question of whether there is a constitutional basis for the exercise of power at the international level which permits the creation of rules engages with a Kelenian perspective of law: the existence of the basic norm at the domestic level creates legitimacy which could affect acts at the international level. Thus, the exercise of power is justified and such acts have authority because of the existence of a basic norm which creates validity for all other norms.[24] Under this theory, constitutional norms, for example, would be the basis of authority in the domestic system

[20] Byers (n 18) 48.

[21] von Bernstorff (n 4) 158 and Koskenniemi (n 19) 181.

[22] James Crawford, *The Creation of States in International Law* (2nd edn, Oxford University Press 2006).

[23] Çali (n 5) 25.

[24] Hans Kelsen, *Pure Theory of Law* (2nd edn, Lawbook Exchange 2005), 199.

because such norms authorise the State to exercise power within certain bounds. On such a reading of the domestic approach, it would appear to lend support to the argument that the source of authority of international law is that of the State; its willing agreement[25] and consent creates authoritative rules because it exercises power derived from the basic norm.

However, this would mean that the internal functioning of States and their internal workings would justify the exercise of power at the international level, which is not always the case. The variations present in domestic law can be overruled at the international level, creating a degree of friction between domestic provisions and international provisions. There are many constitutional systems which never have any impact on international law, and which struggle to even assert their voices on the international stage. At the other end of the scale, there may be actors which lack domestic authority because of the absence of a basic norm, yet can make law at the international level. Luban notes that the problem of consent centres on the expectation of democratic authorisation,[26] but that state consent is not necessarily morally significant where states do not represent their citizenry. However, it does not mean that a domestic regime which lacks authority, under the Kelsenian understanding or otherwise, is incapable of making law at the international level. This was demonstrated earlier, in the context of Libya, where the government had ratified a number of human rights without evidencing domestic authority to do so.

Raz's idea of the power of domestic organs as being purely an internal matter within the confines of the sovereignty of the State would make certain issues purely internal to the State.[27] It is not disputed that internal constitutional matters are dealt with by States, and that State actors should take steps to exercise power in line with the constitutional provisions. As such, constitutional norms, as identifiable basic norms, do not exist outwith the bounds of sovereign nations, even if those nations are not formally recognised as States, and so sovereignty is innately bound in the existence of a domestic legal system. Koskenniemi refers to Kelsen's approach in this respect as the 'legal approach'[28] because it requires that sovereignty be identified as emanating from the domestic law.[29] However, it should be noted that neither sovereignty

[25] Raz, *The Morality of Freedom* (n 11) 337.
[26] Allen Buchanan, *Justice, Legitimacy, and Self-Determination: Moral Foundations for International Law* (Oxford University Press 2003), 65.
[27] Joseph Raz, *Between Authority and Interpretation: On the Theory of Law and Practical Reason* (Oxford University Press 2009), 125.
[28] Koskenniemi (n 19) 228.
[29] von Bernstorff (n 4) 63

nor power should be equated with political authority to act,[30] even at the domestic level. There is thus a clear distinction between the idea of authority, particularly political authority, and the power to make rules. The validity of the rules is clearly at issue where the power to give consent exists without the political authority to make legal rules at the international level.

The character of international law must go beyond a domestic interpretation otherwise its normative value would be undermined,[31] making it no more than an ancillary system to the domestic establishment. To regard it as subordinate to the domestic system would also be considered a 'logical absurdity,' according to Triepel,[32] given that the authority would be derived from the consent of the State; without the State, there could be no consent and thus no authority. Thus, it cannot be held that authority is rooted primarily in the State as, for the system to function, there must be something beyond the domestic level. This mandates some kind of external aspect to the system of international law,[33] where States can form law on the basis of authority beyond the State. The engagement with sovereignty as evidence of the ability of the State to do any more than exercise power is supported by Kelsen, who disregards the existence of sovereignty as a 'fallacy'[34] created for political ends. Others noted that it meant little beyond identifying the rights and duties of States.[35] Kelsen argued for a revision of the concept of sovereignty for this very reason,[36] to distinguish the justification for the exercise of power at the domestic level from that of the creation of rules at the international level.

Because of its failure to be rooted in anything other than domestic law, there had to be something external to the domestic order for international law which conferred legitimacy on the system. His conclusion was that a higher order applied to States, making them equal, and such sovereign equality was the basis on which States were able to justify the creation of rules at the international level. Thus, there is something beyond the State which allows each to participate in the creation of rules in a justifiable way, because of the existence of a hierarchy of rules. Above the States sits the principle of sovereign equality. This would appear to be the hierarchy that Dworkin argues

30 Raz, *The Morality of Freedom* (n 11) 76.
31 Koskenniemi (n 19) 385.
32 von Bernstorff (n 4) 39.
33 Koskenniemi (n 19) 181.
34 Kelsen (n 24) 383
35 Koskenniemi (n 19) 235.
36 von Bernstorff (n 4) 62

cannot be located,[37] although perception of it is required when identifying the source of public international law's authority. Koskenniemi concurs that sovereign equality can have an impact on the validity of rules because of the need to understand how the State has the authority to rule, using this as his classic explanation of how international law is reduced to either apology or utopia.[38] States are equal to one another, because the principle of sovereign equality creates such equality, and this gives States the authority to create law.

That external aspect, or something beyond the mere existence of a sovereign, is problematic. Areas such as the protection of human rights confer political legitimacy, beyond the mere existence of a democratic State.[39] Buchanan goes further than this idea, stating that legitimacy is possible where political power is exercised with a moral justification and that anything beyond this would be considered coercion.[40] He does concede, however, that the international system can attain legitimacy should it protect individual rights.[41] He takes particular issue with the notion of coercive consent, even for the protection of human rights, and cites the use of peace agreements in situations which may be coercive. Although consensual, it could be argued that those who are defeated in an armed conflict would have no choice but to accept, and Buchanan notes that the Vienna Convention accepted consent under duress where there is no violation of the UN Charter.[42] Thus, consent as the basic or super norm of the international system does not really possess a voluntary character[43] and allows stronger States to constrain less powerful States.[44] This form of argumentation is circular and also disregards the use of power to eradicate, to colonialise, through methods of coercive consent. Given the historic use of the UN Charter to support colonialisation via the mandate system, it is not considered sufficiently protective to accept consent under duress on the proviso that the UN Charter would not be violated. The idea that legitimacy rests alone on the protection of individual rights dismisses situations in which rights must be balanced against one another, where there are competing interests, or in situations where the moral justification is questionable. Many invasions of other countries in the twenty-first century have been justified on the basis of the protection of the rights of individuals, in

[37] Çali (n 5) 38.
[38] Koskenniemi (n 19) 282.
[39] Buchanan (n 26) 146.
[40] ibid 152.
[41] ibid 161.
[42] ibid 187.
[43] ibid 187.
[44] ibid 192.

the invaded country or that of the invader, and thus there would need to be a clearer set of conditions as to what a moral justification in this context would entail.

To evade the idea of coercive consent implemented by one or two States, and to protect individuals, perhaps even from their own States, might authority derive from a collective of States, rather than States as individuals? Thus, the consent of one State does not generate authority, but authority may be conferred where the grouping agrees on a particular rule. This would go beyond individual consent and suggest that there are situations in which collective consent may justify the exercise of power. The idea of a collective of States as the source of authority, in which they pool their authority via consent at the international level, is worth briefly exploring. Verdross considered that the UN Charter may be the source of authority primarily because of collective consent.[45] However, Çali then argues that the authority of law is derived from its domestic political authority, but that the collective nature of international law does not confer the same authority and thus it can only ever be guidance.[46] This conflict between the sources of authority as domestic or international is interesting, particularly in light of the example given of the Libyan constitutional provisions earlier in this chapter. Indeed, the presumption of the existence of constitutional norms undermines the universality of this approach; it may be possible that international agreement on rules and treaties is indeed what generates their authority, beyond the domestic conception. This reverts to the international rule of law thesis, using sovereign equality as a rule: the individual States can act in concert at the international level and their agreement confers authority on the laws, beyond a guideline. Using Raz's normative justification, it could be held that authority in the international community could derive from the members themselves recognising that certain burdens need to be imposed for the functioning of the community as a whole.[47] The nature of this idea has already been explored in part by Schucking and Wehberg, who conceived of a 'sphere of will' emanating from each sovereign nation. That sphere, most critically, was independent of the individual community members.[48] Von Bernstorff highlights the value of this and the contribution thereto by Kelsen because of his basic norm.[49] One may also call this the international rule of law, the norm which gives

[45] Çali (n 5) 39.
[46] ibid 92.
[47] Raz, *The Morality of Freedom* (n 11) 71.
[48] von Bernstorff (n 4) 142.
[49] ibid 143.

validity to all other norms and through which the liberty of individual States could be restricted.[50] Thus the international rule of law could possibly be the norm from which the power of the State is restrained and authority is created.

This could be demonstrated through the view of the power of international law, as something to which States wish to adhere, even when it conflicts with their wants or interests. This was discussed by O'Connell[51] in the context of the Bush torture memos.[52] She argues that the administration, in attempting to evade the definition of torture, still wished to comply.[53] In her work, she critiques Goldsmith and Posner, where they argue about international law as a form of coordination, a 'special kind of politics.' Their approach, she states, is a demonstration of how hard it is to dismiss international law.[54] This connects with the ideas of Franck, building on the previous work of Kelsen, Grotius, and many others, who considered the origin of legitimacy to emanate from the community[55] because consent is transcended by other things relevant to international law. International law reflects shared goals, higher aims, and this understanding should enhance its authority.[56] This makes the loss of Morgenthau as an international law scholar all the more tragic, where he considered the law too weak to command respect[57] following his first-hand experience of Nazism. Consequently, he felt that 'the ultimate goal of all men is the quest for power and that security lay only in having greater power than others.'[58] Yet this approach would undermine that argument, as no one State would be considered greater than others and the agreement of all would undermine any one attempt to seek power or dominance, or at least to justify seeking that power or dominance.

Although Kelsen's basic norm as the international rule of law is not conclusively proved here, there is strong evidence to support the idea that consent is not the sole source of authority of international law. Instead, it constitutes an exercise of power with State consent being one element from which it draws authority. However, the legitimate exercise of that power, constrained by something beyond the will of the government, may constitute

50 Koskenniemi (n 19) 239.
51 Mary Ellen O'Connell, *The Power and Purpose of International Law: Insights from the Theory and Practice of Enforcement* (Oxford University Press 2008), 1.
52 Michael P Scharf, 'International Law and the Torture Memos' (2009) 42 Case W Res J Int'l L 321.
53 O'Connell (n 51) 1.
54 ibid 2.
55 ibid 8.
56 ibid 370.
57 ibid 59.
58 ibid 60.

authority. Before discussing the role of morality in constraining the exercise of power, the legitimacy of that exercise will be discussed.

3.3 WHAT ABOUT LEGITIMACY?

The idea of consent being the root of authority at the international level can only really work if consent is deconstructed as an exercise of power and then the power itself is understood as legitimately exercised. Buchanan and Keohane focus on the idea that institutions are legitimate where they have the normative right to rule,[59] restricting themselves to the idea that there should be a domestic basis for legitimacy. Meyer puts forward the idea of normative legitimacy by consent, in that winning power via an election 'makes it easier to wield that power,'[60] although not necessarily more legitimate. However, Besson notes that State consent can be justified as having a key role in international law-making to strengthen its legitimacy.[61] From the current discussion, this would appear to be rather circular in nature and the idea of legitimacy is not greatly furnished beyond the ability to act at the international level. Consent could also be regarded as a method of explaining the morally binding nature of promises, per Raz, although it remains unclear as to how law can bind.

As Besson notes, 'one may indeed consent to do wrong,'[62] and such wrongdoing would not necessarily create legitimacy in other acts. Besson posits a 'revised Razian account to the extent that the main basis of the demand for legitimate authority is reasonable disagreement about how to structure common action when such action is required morally or practically.'[63] As such, legitimacy is more likely to stem from coordinated, potentially institutional action rather than the collective consent of States alone.

However, the idea of coordinated action is not something which would automatically be legitimate. The idea that international law perpetrates the

[59] Allen Buchanan and Robert Keohane, 'The Legitimacy of Global Governance Institutions' 29–57, 29 in Lukas H Meyer (ed), *Legitimacy, Justice and Public International Law* (Cambridge University Press 2009).

[60] Lukas Meyer and Pranay Sanklecha, 'Three Perspectives on the Debate' 1–28, 2 in Lukas H Meyer (ed), *Legitimacy, Justice and Public International Law* (Cambridge University Press 2009).

[61] Samantha Besson, 'State Consent and Disagreement in International Law-Making: Dissolving the Paradox' (2016) 29 LJIL 289, 289.

[62] ibid 289, 300.

[63] ibid 289, 302.

unfairness of an unjust world[64] is discussed by both Butt and Nagel, in which they view international law as a vehicle for the continual degradation of weaker States and individuals. Franck notes the irrelevance of much of the text of the UN Charter to how nations behave in fact, by noting that it would mean little to Martians should they land tomorrow.[65] More critically, however, the system requires something beyond a sovereign, and beyond the UN Charter, to achieve legitimacy. It is interesting that the very beginning of the discipline, in the work of Grotius, that he noted the importance of humanity in the law of nations[66] and the connection between rights and personhood.[67] He goes on to note the importance of the state of right reason and the way in which actions are binding by their command based on certain 'natural' rules.[68] Franck challenges this, however, by noting that there are few questions on 'why these, or any other, rules are or are not, or should or should not be, obeyed.'[69] He points out that 'disobedience is the only norm'[70] and that the idea of government at the national level is challenged by those who protest against human rights abuses in the global order.[71] However, this would accord more with an understanding of authority rooted not in state consent, but in the rights of individuals at the international level. The influence of individual rights, and respect therefore, appears to be key in the understanding of authority in the context of international law. This would take the argument slightly further than a reliance on coordinated action as the basis for legitimacy.

Pellet notes that there is a link between democracy and legitimacy at the domestic level, but less so at the international level, for reasons including the lack of separation of powers.[72] He notes that democracy has absolutely nothing to do with international society, even where the UN exists,[73] and that legitimacy cannot be assimilated with fairness or justice.[74] This would indicate that the domestic system, and the way in which it is run, is of little importance to

64 Daniel Butt, 'Victors' Justice? Historic Injustice and the Legitimacy of International Law' 163–185, 163 in Lukas H Meyer (ed), *Legitimacy, Justice and Public International Law* (Cambridge University Press 2009).

65 Thomas Franck, 'Why a Quest for Legitimacy?' (1987) 21 UC Davis L Rev 535, 546.

66 Hugo Grotius, *The Rights of War and Peace* (Liberty Fund 2005), 9.

67 ibid 19.

68 ibid 21.

69 Franck, 'Why a Quest for Legitimacy?' (n 65) 535, 536.

70 ibid 535, 536.

71 ibid 535, 539.

72 Alain Pellet, 'Legitimacy of Legislative and Executive Actions of International Institutions' 63–82, in Wil Waluchow and Stefan Schiaffra (eds), *The Legacy of Ronald Dworkin* (Oxford University Press 2016), 65

73 ibid 66.

74 ibid 68.

the international order. He continues that an unfair system is not enough to contest its legitimacy[75] and international law is a 'subtle alchemy of a great variety of elements which at the end of the day result in a generalised *opinio juris*, which founds both the efficiency and the legitimacy of the rule of law.'[76] This is therefore a kind of legitimacy, taking account of more than just the domestic system, the fairness of the international system, or morality alone. D'Amato criticises the idea of legitimacy as a benchmark because it is 'hopelessly ambiguous' and is persuaded of the distinction between lawfulness and legitimacy.[77]

Rights alone do not influence the authority of international law; Roughan notes that law is neither tidy nor lonely[78] and is thus directly influenced by other areas, such as politics and morality. On this basis, there ought to be an acknowledgement of the growing influence of international and transnational law as examples of legal systems. Hart's view, that international law was not really law, is no longer relevant[79] where the State has lost its power and where the influence of international and transnational agreements exerts such influence over the domestic legal order.

Based on this, Roughan posits that the existing systems have relative authority; that is, authority relative to one another.[80] This aims to address the weakness of Raz's service conception account, which is rendered, in her eyes, 'unstable' by the existence of plural orders which may command different levels of authority.[81] However, the instability of Raz's service conception is not fully evidenced, as the balance of reasons for which one may act allows the engagement with plural orders of authority. This can be seen through the interesting division between those who have authority and those who are sovereign, in that those who are legitimately sovereign may be separate from those who have legitimate authority.[82] Specifically, now that the Westphalian order has eroded somewhat, there is a greater degree of separation between the two: sovereignty is no longer complete and absolute, but rather dependent on external factors,[83] such as the flow of capital. Raz uses Shapiro's work to

75 ibid 81–82.
76 ibid 82.
77 Anthony D'Amato, 'On the Legitimacy of International Institutions' 83–92, in Wil Waluchow and Stefan Schiaffra (eds), *The Legacy of Ronald Dworkin* (Oxford University Press 2016), 83.
78 Nicole Roughan, *Authorities: Conflicts, Cooperation and Transnational Legal Theories* (Oxford University Press 2013), 1.
79 ibid 2.
80 ibid 3.
81 ibid 8.
82 ibid 12.
83 ibid 14.

indicate that practical authority is where one has the normative power to change another's normative relations.[84] It is neither coercive nor influential but has the power to effect change. It is difficult to understand this third way in practice, however: if something is neither coercive nor influential, would it have any effect at all? The power to change reasons because one ought to on the basis of morality is either coercive: you consider your actions or person bad as a consequence of not obeying the directive, or influential: you want to be a good person. A third way would be corrective in the sense of absolute power, which would undermine entirely the idea of autonomy.

Roughan also references the work of Neil Walker, who speaks of a 'fragmented, fluid and contested configuration of authority,'[85] meaning that legitimacy and authority remain plural, with no single understanding of what constitutes an authoritative, legitimate order. Both Roughan and Walker converge on this idea of plurality, with many global orders existing in parallel, and sometimes competing for primacy, at other times allowing for the possibility of overlap without one having to be subjugated or subsumed by the other.[86] This should be acknowledged by authorities working in the same domain, who ought to find either borders for their authorities, which is unlikely given the near-constant struggle to obtain and maintain power, or establish hierarchies.[87] The existence of a plurality of authorities creates a degree of difficulty in identifying which authorities ought to be followed.

The relationship between authorities, as a method of measuring legitimacy, is perhaps something which supports the idea of consent, in that States will sometimes possess authority and may relinquish it in other situations. There is a relationship here between this work and the work of Alter, Helfer, and Madsen, in that the authority of law may be dependent on the context in which it operates.[88] The utility of these ideas is their breadth: it aids in our understanding of public international law more generally, in that its authority may emanate from different places and spaces depending on the way in which power is being exercised.

Buchanan's work focuses on these ideas well; he makes four points in relation to legitimacy and the international system. In one of the four points, he cites the critical aspect of justice as a goal, support by human rights, and the

84 ibid 20 and see Shapiro also.
85 Neil Walker, 'Beyond Boundary Disputes and Basic Grids: Mapping the Global Disorder of Normative Orders' (2008) 6 IJCL 373.
86 Roughan (n 78) 46.
87 ibid.
88 Madsen et al. (n 10).

importance of securing human rights to attain legitimacy.[89] Although discussed in the context of self-determination, he makes several key connections between the idea of legitimacy and the role of rights and justice. Legitimate exercises of power are only possible where the goal is to secure justice; States cannot act legitimately in the international sphere without having regard for the human rights of those over whom they exert power. The notion of human rights is thus central to the justice-based international system.[90] The concept of procedural justice is also a goal, because is constitutes a 'moral target and therefore justice and peace are not necessarily in conflict'.[91]

This connects well to Thomas Pogge's idea that an unfair global system inflicts harm and therefore 'justice (should be) a goal of international law.'[92] This provides a timely reminder that structures are created by people and thus do not require automatic acceptance by other States or by the community in general. States and their acts do not require acceptance, nor is here an obligation to approve all the ways in which they exercise power. Consequently, the legitimate exercise of power at the international level may depend on the context in which it is exercised, it may acquire authority, or have its authority challenged when acting in a number of different spheres, but it cannot claim authority if it does not serve the aim of providing justice and respecting rights. This hints at a moral dimension to the exercise of power, and one which has been considered by many scholars in the area. The question of how morality affects this exercise is thus relevant, as a potential source of authority for international law.

3.4 THE ROLE OF MORALITY

The role of morality in conferring legitimacy on State actors in international law, and thus offering their acts a degree of authority, is complex. Buchanan's ideas, discussed earlier, relate to the role of morality as a justification for certain practices. He laments the lack of application of political philosophy to international relations,[93] and what he considers to be a lack of institutional moral theorising.[94] However, this presumes the ability of the State to act and to conduct its affairs in an autonomous fashion. There is evidence to support

89 Buchanan (n 26) 43.
90 ibid 48.
91 ibid 50.
92 ibid 54.
93 ibid 12.
94 ibid 13.

the idea that sovereign states are mere by-products[95] of the exercise of power and thus lack the necessary autonomy to act. Rulers, actors, therefore, are critical at the international level; the existence of State sovereignty is, in the view of Krasner, 'organized hypocrisy.'[96] Cogently, he cites the military intervention in Libya in 2011[97] as a conflict which will not change the international balance of power; it does not reflect how things happened previously. 'The Americans and Europeans engaged in air strikes without having confidence in, or much knowledge about, the nature of the Libyan opposition.'[98] What sort of system, what sort of morality, can be said to exist where the international system relies on certain actors behaving as they see fit, without having even the knowledge of the consequences of their actions? There is a gap between the authority to act in areas which will affect the interests of rich, powerful countries (or areas in which rulers have an interest) and areas which lack the connection to the rich and powerful which offers protection.

This makes the reading of morality into the system particularly interesting: Dworkin's argument is against a legal positivist understanding of international law and in favour of a moralised reading, focusing on the idea of a system.[99] Yet the system alluded to would not support acts such as military intervention in Libya in 2011. Buchanan's idea is that incoherent approaches thus far have undermined international practice in certain areas,[100] and it is difficult to disagree. The role of power, rather than authority, has been used at the domestic level, according to Krasner to affect 'domestic authority structures'[101] too. His allusion here is to wars of invasion which have then been used to undermine or replace domestic authority figures, which has become something of a feature of Western military exercises in the twenty-first century. The existence of States which can be invaded and occupied in a successful way

95 Peter J Katzenstein, 'States and Power as Ur-Force: Domestic Traditions and Embedded Actors in World Politics' 139–156, 140 in Martha Finnemore and Judith Goldstein (eds), *Back to Basics: State Power in a Contemporary World* (Oxford University Press 2013).

96 ibid 139–156, 147.

97 See, among others, Hanspeter Mattes, 'Libya since 2011: Political Transformation and Violence' (2016) 23 Middle East Policy 59.

98 Stephen Krasner, 'New Terrains: Sovereignty and Alternative Conceptions of Power' 339–358, 339–340 in Martha Finnemore and Judith Goldstein (eds), *Back to Basics: State Power in a Contemporary World* (Oxford University Press 2013).

99 Thomas Christiano and Ronald Dworkin, 'State Consent and Progressive Cosmopolitanism' 49–69 in Wil Waluchow and Stefan Schiaffra (eds), *The Legacy of Ronald Dworkin* (Oxford University Press 2016), 49.

100 Buchanan (n 26) 11.

101 Krasner (n 98) 339–358, 355.

reflects, in his view, 'the structural power of the West, the extent to which sovereignty is the only universally recognized way to organize political life.'[102] On this basis, there is a strong link between sovereignty and authority, sovereignty being the main way in which power is exercised at the international level. The power they have can be compulsory[103] or institutional,[104] but it is undeniable. It is through this structural power that States can claim their authority. There is little mention, in such cases, of the role of morality and a greater focus on the ability of the State to act. Arguably, this is a more universal way of viewing the exercise of power at the international level; there is a lack of focus on when things go well and when States can make treaties, or when *opinio juris* can be correctly discerned so as to appreciate which rule ought to be applied. Authority in this case follows sovereignty; sovereignty and the power associated with one's sovereign state permit the actor or ruler to rule in the way they see fit, without regard for any external rule.

Criddle and Fox-Decent provide an interesting account of State authority alternative to this, noting that sovereign authority depends on the State, but that the authority to act is rooted in morality.[105] Their work holds that the basic rules of dignity and humanity are 'constitutive of state sovereignty.'[106] As such, States which do not conduct their actions according to a recognised morality in dealing with their populations lack the sovereignty to act in international law. This idea has been argued before, in a more fundamental way, when Butler noted that the 'advancement of human dignity should … guide all exercises of authority and power.'[107] The State's authority must then derive, not from its ability to guarantee control, but from the way in which it treats its population. Adherence to the rules of basic dignity would then create the competence on the part of the State to make law at the international level because of both its democratic mandate to do so[108] and its ability to secure that mandate by respecting the rights and voice of its polity. Fox-Decent, individually, proposes that authority is justified on moral grounds.[109] He checks Hobbes as identifying authority as a right, and connected acts by someone

[102] ibid 339–358, 356.
[103] ibid 339–358, 347.
[104] ibid 339–358, 348.
[105] Criddle and Fox-Decent (n 6).
[106] ibid 29.
[107] Israel de Jesus Butler, 'Securing Human Rights in the Face of International Integration' (2011) 60 ICLQ 125.
[108] Koskenniemi (n 19) 234.
[109] Evan Fox-Decent, *Sovereignty's Promise: The State as Fiduciary* (Oxford University Press 2011), 3.

who has the right to do so.[110] There are no obligations under natural law because only the sovereign has authority[111] but the sovereignty has a fiduciary duty in respect of its people which it then carries to the international system.[112] The fiduciary relationship arises from sovereignty, because the State has the monopoly on force, *per* Alter,[113] although countries which have been the subject of campaigns by NATO may disagree, given the force that it may unify and deploy. The automatic nature of trust marks a relationship of power.[114]

The truth would appear to lie somewhere between the two extremes; based on the arguments by Fox-Decent and Criddle, the State may have more or less authority depending on the way in which it treats its population, but it will also have more or less power depending on its history, geopolitics, and natural resources, among other elements. Its authority and power are connected, and morality does play a role in the way in which it can exercise this power. In the context of international law, Koskenniemi notes that 'if law had no relation to power and political fact, it would be a form of natural morality, a closed normative code which would pre-exist the opinions or interests of individual States.'[115] Naturalism as the source of authority is not being argued here; as Kammerhofer points out that natural law makes it very difficult for international law to be considered valid law,[116] because it does not conform to reason on each occasion of its application. This can be seen very clearly in the example given of military intervention in Libya in 2011, earlier, and also in the example of 'full naturalism' offered by Koskenniemi: he highlights this in a case from the International Court of Justice as one such example, the Anglo-Norwegian Fisheries case.[117] In this case, the Norwegian authorities delineated its territory in the North Sea using a set of baselines and decreed them so in 1935. Having applied them consistently for many years, the British government then objected that the Norwegian delineation should be accepted as the legal rule as they had not accepted it. The Court held that the British activities in the area meant that its government would have been aware of the way in which the borders were drawn and, accordingly, that they had tacitly agreed to

[110] ibid 9.
[111] ibid 14–15.
[112] ibid 22.
[113] ibid 29.
[114] ibid 108.
[115] Koskenniemi (n 19).
[116] Jorg Kammerhofer, *Uncertainty in International Law: A Kelsenian Perspective* (Routledge 2011) 224.
[117] Fisheries case *(UK v Norway)* [1951] ICJ Rep 116.

the borders delineated by Norway. Koskenniemi argues that this is 'indistinguishable from full naturalism,'[118] as the Court sets out the idea of to what the British government have consented. This was based on the Court's reasoning and a strong argument that the UK ought to have been fully aware of the way in which maritime delineation was carried out.

However, the argument here is not focused on subsuming the Court's judgment for the UK's judgment: it concerned the acquiescence of the UK government to the Norwegian approach to delimitation. Koskenniemi argues that the Court used its own logic to determine the agreement of the UK, but interestingly, it appears to be rooted more in the acceptance of the UK of the rule, or the failure to object. For the purposes of understanding natural law and morality, the case here takes a different approach arguably because of the equality of sovereignty between the UK and Norway. It is possible to apply the rules in a logical fashion because they are equal in power, developed, and arguably in possession of the same sort of authority. In such a situation, the role of power can be set aside, and the case can be analysed, one might say, clearly. The rules can be applied, logic can be used, and natural law can be considered part of the method to provide a deeper understanding of the rule. The extent to which international law can fit into a natural law conception is limited, outwith the clear use of basic reason, or logic, as a source of rules. It is also difficult to determine the extent to which international law could ever have a source of authority that would satisfy natural law, and even reason can be unseated by power and politics.

Such an approach is problematic, but it also defeats the claim of naturalism and natural law as a good fit for international law. There may be good reasons for the Court's decision, based on how the UK ought to have understood the boundaries of its territories, but the reason is not objective, not connected to an eternal law or deity, and the reasoning is not clearly found in objective principles. Indeed, it seems more guided by a broad sense of fairness than a specific rule governing the situation. Thus, there is a lack of clearly identifiable authority in international law, from a natural law perspective, and one which consequently undermines its nature as law, and makes it seem more likely a conduit for political decisions. These decisions have little impact, as demonstrated earlier, where the entities are equal in power, status, and wealth, but have a much greater, graver impact where a power asymmetry exists between the two entities. This is relevant to certain areas of public international law, and most significantly in international criminal law.

[118] Koskenniemi (n 19) 297.

The role of morality in the authority of public international law is therefore limited; the question of power is much more significant and the existence of a sovereign state as a conduit for that power allows for a system in which power can be exercised. Those entities exercising their powers can be restrained, to an extent, by the existence of rights and the requirements of a moral order, but there is more than a degree of incoherence in the results of such exercises. The power asymmetries which exist undermine arguments of morality and naturalism; these appear only to apply in any concrete way to cases or situations concerning those equal in power. Morality is a facet of authority in public international law, but not one which has any great bearing. The role of rights, and the protection thereof, would appear to restrain States more effectively but in certain cases, there is no match for political power. The argument remains, however, that such exercises of power lack authority. The ability to carry out acts of violence with impunity confers neither legitimacy nor authority on those acts nor on the actors who commit them.

3.5 CONCLUSION

At the international level, the competence to issue rules[119] is viewed as a critical aspect of legal authority, in the context of public international law. Legitimate authority is thus connected to the existence of an order which is supported by a domestic, authoritative order: the connection between the domestic order and the international order is critical, and authoritative international law can only be made where the domestic governments possess the requisite authority. The authority of States can be used as a means to understand the authority of the rules themselves, by which their consent confers authority as a legitimate exercise of their power. However, consent is not the only source of authority, and other aspects of power at the international level can influence the authority of certain acts. The role of morality would arguably confer authority on the acts of such States. However, that presumes the significance, and equality, of sovereign States throughout the world.

Using political theory, the above discussion notes that sovereignty can offer privilege, as well as connote power in certain circumstances. Thus, the actors who exercise that power are more influential than the consent they confer on behalf of the State itself. That does not mean, however, that their acts have authority, but the way in which they conduct themselves can influence international law. This is one of the main issues with a State-based system.

[119] ibid 234.

The role of morality, thus, should offer a restraint on such exercises of power, yet there is a lack of regard for morality in such circumstances. The role of external normative orders is not demonstrated well; even the use of naturalism as a source of logic is not evidenced well in the international system. The respect for rights at the international level resurges as a source of authority and would appear to be the most convincing way in which authority is conferred. The problematic aspect to this, which remains, is the way in which exercises of power which lack legitimacy continue to influence and change the rules of the international system by constituting State practice. Through the characterisation of such exercises of power as lacking legitimacy, it is meant that they are not rooted in authority, but rather the ability of the State to act. No underlying justification is present; the State may pursue its own interests because of a lack of central authority and the inability, or lack of will, of stronger States to restrain its actions. These become, thus, mere exercises of power. The development in such cases may have a longer-term effect on the legitimacy of acts, meaning that today's dealings may lack authority, while conferring it on tomorrow's acts.

The role of sovereignty and the human rights dimension of international law continues to influence the question of authority at the international level. The next chapter develops these ideas further in relation to international criminal law specifically. The idea of international criminal law as a discrete area will be examined, including the question of the authority of the ICC. This includes an examination of the jurisdiction of the Court, and the question of whether its authority is sufficiently evidenced in different areas. This includes in situations where power is exercised by the UNSC where it initiates investigations, as well as a further examination of the role of power politics as the alleged source of authority, to determine whether such situations are reduced to an exercise of power rather than authoritative acts.

4

The Authority of International Criminal Law

4.1 INTRODUCTION

As a branch of public international law, international criminal law (ICL) has its roots in the same sources as public international law: it has been devised by States, based on their practice and acknowledgement of existing rules, as well as consensus on the definitions of specific international crimes. Historically, agreements have been formed to underscore its rules and to codify certain elements of the system, such as defences. The London Agreement, for example, set out the crimes which were within the jurisdiction of the Nuremberg Tribunal, and the respective statutes for the International Criminal Tribunals for both Rwanda and the former Yugoslavia had a similar task in delineating the content of the criminal law applicable by the tribunals. The main distinction between ICL and other areas of public international law, such as the law of sea, is the way in which ICL has a partly compulsory jurisdiction: the question of jurisdiction is typically settled during the drafting of the Statute or Agreement, and the law then applies. There are no examples of negotiating with those who have been accused in situations relating to ad hoc or war crimes tribunals to determine whether they agree that the law should apply to them. It equally did not matter whether the States of the nationals accused agreed with the establishment of tribunals. Thus, the question of jurisdiction of the subject matter is settled during the drafting of the Statute, be it Rome or for Rwanda, and the personal and geographical jurisdiction would also have previously been set within the Statute or agreement.

However, the creation of the ICC was different. It had not been created in response to a specific situation or tragedy, and the negotiations were not completed with a view to focusing on a particular context. It was thus more straightforward, in that the law could be set out without concern for a particular set of individuals accused, and more complicated, in that general rules were being created for situations that the States Parties acknowledged could apply to them. The initial criminal tribunals during the Second World War justified their jurisdiction with reference to the necessity of their intervention because of the failure of the German domestic courts to prosecute (or to consider illegal) the acts of those who had coordinated many atrocities during the Second World War. It is not immediately apparent that this justification accords authority. Moreover, since the ICC lacked an immediate justification for action, it is equally unclear that the roots of the authority of ICL and the present system under the ICC possess clear authority. Since the project of international criminal justice has been in motion since the inception of the UN,[1] the roots of the authority of the ICL require further elaboration.

The basis of the authority of ICL shares some of the features of the authority of public international law, in that positivism and natural law play a role. However, the role of natural law has been overstated, in that the crimes themselves appear to be drawn from both natural law and positive domestic criminal law. ICL also places limits on what States may legally do without requiring their consent: the law may be broken, even where the Court does not have jurisdiction. The example of aggression is particularly interesting here, in that the definition was agreed in 1974[2] but only fell within the jurisdiction of the Court in 2015.[3] Consensus on the definition existed, but consent to include it as a crime within the Statute was lacking. The existence of the law without the ability of the ICC to prosecute is demonstrated amply by the invasion of Ukraine by Russia in 2022.[4] Although the ICC now has jurisdiction over the crime of aggression, the Russian invasion of Ukraine cannot be prosecuted there without an amendment to the Rome Statute.[5] As a non-State Party, only a UNSC referral could allow the amendment incorporating the crime of aggression to be enforced against Russia. In contrast to previous tribunals, there is an abundance of codified law, but no possibility of prosecution without the intervention of the UNSC.

As such, the Rome Statute has changed the way in which ICL operates. It clearly outlines the crimes within the jurisdiction of the Court, enunciating all of those contained within the previous Statutes of the criminal tribunals, as well as elucidating concepts which were not previously outlined by these

1 M Cherif Bassiouni, *The Legislative History of the International Criminal Court* (Ardsley 2005).
2 United Nations General Assembly Resolution 3314 (XXIX) (Definition of Aggression) A/RES/3314 (Document), 14 December 1974.
3 Article 8*bis*, Rome Statute.
4 Russian Invasion of Ukraine, 'Ukraine War in Maps: Tracking the Russian Invasion' BBC News.
5 Prosecuting Putin for His Crime of Aggression against Ukraine: Part One | OHRH (ox.ac.uk).

Statutes. These concepts included the crime of sexual slavery and the codification of the concept of defences. The jurisdiction of the Court is also set out by the Statute, and it equally varies from previously established practice. The UNSC may now make referrals to it, justified by the mantle of peace and security under which it operates, meaning that ICL can be applied without the consent and engagement of States. State Party referrals of a third State have a similar impact. In this way, the Rome Statute breaks new ground in a way which has not really been discussed from an authority perspective; it takes the idea of authoritative jurisdiction from previous tribunals and extends it on the grounds of international criminal justice. It also acquires jurisdiction from the exercise of referrals by the UNSC, justified by its UN Charter mandate of maintaining international peace and security.

This chapter will explore the roots of the authority of ICL, including the question of the authority of the ICC. Authority at the international level is delineated by the jurisdiction of the Court, which authorises it to prosecute those who fall within its jurisdiction. Jurisdiction, at the international level, typically engages the idea of consent. For criminal law, this is not precisely the case, and for ICL in particular, the issue of autonomy is contentious. Firstly, criminalisation of the acts themselves constrain individual autonomy. Secondly, the nature of the jurisdiction of the Court, which would typically be predicated on consent, is based on grounds beyond that, including the potential for the UNSC to make a referral to the ICC. This chapter will therefore look at the authority in general of ICL and the authority of previous international criminal tribunals. The next part will examine the jurisdiction of the Court and the way in which it goes beyond the consent of the parties via, for example, UNSC referrals. The role of power politics will then be discussed, before moving on to the question of sovereignty in the next chapter.

4.2 THE ROOTS OF THE AUTHORITY OF ICL

The authority of ICL raises different questions from that of general international law, and yet the issue has not been dealt with in much detail. General texts on the ICC focus on analysing the law itself[6] and there is little discussion around the constitution of international criminal tribunals as an exercise of

6 Otto Triffterer (ed), *Commentary on the Rome Statute of the International Criminal Court* (Beck Hart Nomos 2008); Roy Lee (ed), *The International Criminal Court: The Making of the Rome Statute* (Kluwer Law International 1999); Ilias Bantekas, *International Criminal Law* (Hart 2010); and William Schabas, *The International Criminal Court: A Commentary on the Rome Statute* (Oxford University Press 2010).

power. The purpose of the Court and tribunals tends to be presumed, as a means of achieving justice, and there is little discussion of their authority in general. Although there is evidence to support the existence of international criminal tribunals prior to 1945,[7] the emergence of ICL as a system began in 1945 with the Nuremberg trials, and the subsequent proposals for an international criminal court.[8] The basis for the Nuremberg trials was not really explored in much detail, although there was some reference made to the intention to find an alternative to summary execution. Prior to the end of the war, the declaration issued following the Moscow Conference in 1943 noted:

> Germans who take part in wholesale shooting of Polish officers or in the execution of French, Dutch, Belgian or Norwegian hostages, of Cretan peasants, or who have shared in slaughters inflicted on the people of Poland or in territories of the Soviet Union which are now being swept clear of the enemy, will know they will be brought back to the scene of their crimes and judged on the spot by the peoples whom they have outraged.[9]

Similarly, the London Conference discussions had noted the commitment of the US government to try the Nazi war criminals[10] and the major issues, relayed by Justice Jackson, were focused on the way in which the individuals were to be tried, taking account of the different legal systems and approaches to criminal trials. Similarly, the burgeoning UN Human Rights Committee was focused on the rules regarding the trials, rather than the way in which the Allied powers were able to construct such an enterprise as a legitimate exercise of their authority.[11] Instead, the traditions, customs, and rules of the domestic setting were used as the legal basis of the trials,[12] confirming the positivist origins of ICL and acknowledging the way in which it represents a 'fusion' of domestic and international law.[13] There is little written on the justification of the trials as an exercise of power. Instead, there tends to be allusion to the

7 Gordon Gregory, 'The Trial of Peter von Hagenbach' in Kevin Heller and Gerry Simpson (eds), *The Hidden Histories of War Crimes Trials* (Oxford University Press 2013).

8 Quincy Wright, 'The Proposal for an International Criminal Court' (1952) 46 AJIL 60.

9 https://avalon.law.yale.edu/wwii/moscow.asp.

10 International Conference on Military Trials: London, 1945, Preface, John Jackson, Washington 1947.

11 Margaret E McGuinness, 'Peace v. Justice: The Universal Declaration of Human Rights and the Modern Origins of the Debate' (2011) 35 Dip His 749.

12 International Conference on Military Trials: London, 1945, Preface, John Jackson, Washington 1947.

13 Ilias Bantekas refers to ICL as a 'fusion' of domestic criminal law and public international law; see Bantekas (n 6).

notion that the trials were created as part of the responsibility of the newly created UN to maintain peace and security and 'to bring war criminals to justice,' per the preamble to the London Agreement. Questions regarding the legitimacy of ICL continue to be asked,[14] particularly where there was no clear explanation of the roots of the authority for the creation of the trials. Although there is repeated mention of the interests of justice, the only authorisation appears to come from the UN Charter, as a collective entity which was empowered to deliver justice and maintain peace.

The justification of the Nuremberg trials via the UN Charter was stated clearly in the London Agreement,[15] to which the Charter of the International Military Tribunal (IMT) was annexed. The UN Charter has also been the primary method of justification for subsequent tribunals, for the former Yugoslavia and Rwanda, as part of its Chapter VII powers.[16] Chapter VII has also been used as the basis for agreements between the UN and domestic governments to establish hybrid tribunals, such as the Special Court for Sierra Leone[17] and the Special Tribunal for Lebanon.[18] The UN's power to do so could be identified in two ways: firstly, as that of an international institution empowered with the ability to act as it sees fit or, in the alternative, as a collective which acts through the authority of its members. The two ideas, although close in nature, are distinct because the authority of the former would stand alone, even where individual States' interests were perhaps challenged, while the latter sources its authority from that of domestic governments. The authority of the international institution as an independent entity could be regarded as compelling. It acts under the Charter, and it represents both customary international law as well as State consent. The role of the UN, as an institution which is key to both the recognition of States as well as the international system as a whole, indicates that it possesses the legitimacy of an independent institution. It goes beyond mere consent because it upholds the international order. However, without a Kelsenian basic norm, or a reliance on the international order as distinct, the UN's legitimacy as an international institution cannot go beyond the Charter. In the second instance, the question of the UN reflecting, in a way, the authority of its constituents is possibly a clearer way of identifying its authority. It acts because the UN is empowered by its members to maintain international peace and

[14] William Schabas, 'Victor's Justice: Selecting "Situations" at the International Criminal Court' (2010) 43 JMLR 535.

[15] London Agreement, 8 August 1945, preamble.

[16] UNSC Resolution 827 of 25 May 1993 S/RES/827 and UNSC Resolution 955 of 8 November 1994 S/RES/955.

[17] UNSC Resolution 1315 of 10 August 2002 S/RES/1315.

[18] UNSC Resolution 1757 of 30 May 2007 S/RES/1757.

security under the UN Charter, and thus it can create such tribunals. However, this raises an interesting question regarding the interests of States. In particular, the ICC's power to investigate the behaviour of non-States Parties[19] raises questions about the role of State consent.

In public international law, as discussed earlier, the idea of State consent can be considered to play a role in the authority of the law. However, it is not the only source of authority because of the way in which power affects the ability of certain States to act. The power that States have can either constrain them, in the case of less powerful States, or enable them, in the case of more powerful States. The authority their acts have thus depends on the power they exercise and then whether such acts may affect *opinio juris* in the future. International law in general is always vulnerable to the influence of economically and politically emboldened States.[20] The current authority of law does not derive, however, entirely from the power they wield, or their decision to act. The authority of ICL is thus based in part on State consent because of the authority required to create the Rome Statute.

There would appear to be two key sources of authority for ICL: the UN Charter and State consent. However, reliance on these alone is problematic in almost every example given above of an international criminal tribunal or court. In the case of both Rwanda and former Yugoslavia, the tribunals were established entirely by the UNSC, with the tribunal for the former Yugoslavia having had primacy over any domestic court. The original Tribunal, Nuremberg, did not request the consent of all States Parties involved in the Second World War. In the case of the ICC, there are several States who continue to avoid signing the Statute and remain outwith its jurisdiction under the Statute. The role of the UN is even more visible in these cases because it is still possible to prosecute a State Party which has not formally undertaken the commitments contained within the Rome Statute, where a referral has been made by the UNSC.

There is a limitation placed directly on the establishment of tribunals which engage the international community as a collective, in which the role of State consent is limited because one cannot guarantee that the State in question, when accused of international crimes, would consent to the establishment of a tribunal. The UN's power to establish a tribunal flows directly from the Charter, which also functions as the source of its authority. The practice of

19 Luigi Condorelli and Annalisa Ciampi, 'Comments on the UNSC Referral of the Situation in Darfur to the ICC' (2005) 3 JICJ 590; Dapo Akande, 'The Legal Nature of Security Council Referrals to the ICC and Its Impact on Al-Bashir's Immunities' (2009) 7 JICJ 333.

20 *See* P Sands, *Lawless Word: Making and Breaking Global Rules* (Penguin 2006).

making referrals, however, presents an issue of authority beyond that of both State consent and the Charter. This is primarily because of the potential abuses of power which could occur, by way of politically motivated referrals.[21] This exercise of power obscures the Court's authority; without a clear understanding of what sort of authority the Court has, or how it may be described, it may never be able to disentangle itself from the perception that it functions for the interests of the powerful, rather than for universal values. The ICC may also be vulnerable to abuses of power by those who harbour neo-colonial intentions, a greater risk where certain countries have UNSC privileges and permanent positions.[22]

Other considerations, such as the interests of justice and the protection of rights, must also play a role in determining whether the power has been exercised legitimately. Although certain States may have vetoes and although the UNSC may make referrals, there should be a justification for doing so which goes beyond the Charter itself, and beyond the geopolitical interests of the UNSC. A reliance on the dispensing of justice and a focus on the protection of individual rights appears to be critical: in both the resolutions establishing the tribunal for Rwanda and the former Yugoslavia,[23] the aim of maintaining peace and security is achieved by creating a tribunal to deliver justice. The requirement of justice as part of its mandate for peace and security is key.

The ICC has now undertaken the task of international criminal prosecutions for crimes committed beyond 2002. For this reason, and to better understand the authority of ICL, it is worth examining its jurisdiction and how this relates to the authority of its acts.

4.3 JURISDICTION OF THE ICC AS ITS PRIMARY EXERCISE OF AUTHORITY

The ICC exercises authority, primarily, via its jurisdiction. Its jurisdiction may be 'triggered' in three ways,[24] meaning that an investigation can commence.

[21] Darryl Robinson 'Inescapable Dyads: Why the International Criminal Court Cannot Win' (2015) 28 LJIL 323, 327.

[22] Jochen Von Bernstorff, 'Authority Monism in International Organisations' in Joana Mendes and Ingo Venzke (eds), *Allocating Authority: Who Should Do What in European and International Law?* (Hart 2018), 104.

[23] UNSC Resolution 827 of 25 May 1993 S/RES/827 and UNSC Resolution 955 of 8 November 1994 S/RES/955.

[24] Dominic McGoldrick, 'The International Criminal Court: An End to Impunity?' (1999) 8 CLR 627, 640; *See also* Kerstin Blome and Nora Makard, '"Contested Collisions": Conditions for a Successful Collision Management – The Example of Article 16 of the Rome Statute' (2016) 29 LJIL 551; Robinson (n 21) 323, 327.

The first is via a referral from a State Party,[25] the second is where the Prosecutor begins an investigation on their own initiative,[26] and the third is where there has been a referral from the UNSC.[27] The third way expands the jurisdiction of the Court and raises a question of consent where the State is considered a 'failed State' or where the polity has not elected those who possess the power to govern.[28] The authority for the first two is founded on State authority, while referrals from the UNSC relate to the power exercised under the UN Charter. Following the triggering of jurisdiction, the preconditions for jurisdiction are then examined to determine whether the situation itself can be considered within the jurisdiction of the Court.

The Court's jurisdiction is permitted by the triggering mechanisms.[29] Where the referral is made by a State Party, it would indicate that consent is the root of authority, unless the situation referred lies outwith its boundaries. However, the most controversial of the three is undoubtedly the ability of the UNSC to make referrals.[30] As noted by Bekou and Cryer, the ability of the UNSC to make referrals in this way has extended the reach of the Rome Statute beyond previous Statutes and laws on international criminal tribunals.[31] As part of their discussion, they note that the Court could not have been endowed with universal jurisdiction[32] despite the inherent weaknesses[33] this has created in its jurisdiction. The UNSC's power to make referrals is a compromise between universal jurisdiction and the requirement of consent from every single State in the world, in a manner reminiscent of the UN Charter. States would usually offer permission, but there is the possibility that the UNSC could intervene where it considers the situation to be a threat to international peace and security, particularly in the context of aggression.[34] However, the basis on which the UNSC would claim jurisdiction is entirely distinct from that of criminal jurisdiction: it is acting, under the auspices of the UN Charter, to maintain international peace and security. Its controversy

25 Article 13(a), Rome Statute.

26 ibid.

27 Article 13(b), Rome Statute.

28 Marko Milanovic, 'Is the Rome Statute Binding on Individuals?' (2011) 9 JICJ 25.

29 Article 13, Rome Statute.

30 Article 13(b), Rome Statute; *see* Akande (n 19) 333.

31 Olympia Bekou and Robert Cryer, 'The International Criminal Court and Universal Jurisdiction: A Close Encounter?' (2007) 56 ICLQ 49.

32 ibid 49, 68.

33 ibid 49, 52.

34 Chapter VII, United Nations Charter 1945; *see* Daniel Nsereko, 'The ICC and Complementarity in Principle' (2013) 26 LJIL 427, 430.

stems from the fact that this form of jurisdiction goes beyond the reasoning for criminal jurisdiction, at either the national or international level and seeks to derive authority from the UN Charter. This could be argued as valid given the historical basis of ICL, principally from the perspective of the ad hoc tribunals for the former Yugoslavia and Rwanda, both of which were established under the powers afforded by Chapter VII of the UN Charter.

Universal jurisdiction would typically acquire authority from the State, which could justify the exercise of jurisdiction through the ratification of certain transnational treaties, guaranteeing the prosecution of those who violate the norms within them. For example, States are authorised by the UN Convention against Torture to prosecute instances of torture domestically. Thus, the source of authority would be based on the State's authority to ratify treaties. There would also be a criminal law basis for the exercise of jurisdiction: torture is considered a crime and the justifications for criminal prosecution, which were discussed in previous chapters, would apply here. Despite the crimes being rooted in international law, the exercise of jurisdiction is purely domestic. However, the exercise of power via referrals from the UNSC claims authority on a different basis. The maintenance of international peace and security is the bedrock of the UNSC's powers under Chapter VII of the Charter and forms the basis of the Court's jurisdiction when a referral is made. This would indicate that the source of authority is the Charter, and public international law more generally. As discussed earlier, this form of authority can be problematic. Given the position of the permanent five members of the UNSC, and their power to make referrals, it is not clear that their exercise of power in this way would always be considered legitimate. Indeed, there may be situations in which referrals are not made for political reasons, undermining the authority of the power to act.

Such situations in which referrals are not made may be because the States accused are perhaps members of the P-5, or because there are geopolitical reasons for a member not wishing to make a referral. The UNSC referrals can be vetoed by any one member, meaning that action could be stymied despite a clear threat to international peace and security. Among other things, there is a clear issue with moving the jurisdictional provisions out of the realm of criminal law, with its various justifications for action, and into the sphere of power politics at the UN, where justice may not be dispensed on a fair and equal basis. This also challenges the early points on sovereign equality, as all States are not created equal within the ambit of the UNSC. A clear example of the failure to refer is provided by the situation in Syria since 2014, which the UNSC has refused to refer to the ICC because of the failure of Russia and

China to approve the action.[35] This demonstrates the difficulty presented by relying on the maintenance of peace and security to guarantee justice for the victims of serious violations of ICL.

However, if a referral is made, States are unable to escape it; they cannot evade the authority of the Court where the UNSC has referred the situation. However, there are practical ways to undermine the authority of the Court. For example, it could avoid cooperation and undermine access to evidence, as well as encourage non-cooperation by members of its government and key witnesses. Be that as it may, referrals are relatively rare. Only two situations, the alleged genocide and crimes against humanity in Darfur and the armed conflict in Libya since 2011, have been referred thus far. As noted earlier, an attempt to refer Syria to the ICC was vetoed by China and Russia in 2014.[36] The text of the referrals urges the States at hand to offer their full cooperation with the Court,[37] as a tacit acknowledgement of how difficult asserting authority in these cases may be.

The preconditions of the jurisdiction should then be met once jurisdiction has been triggered. For the Court to proceed with an investigation, it must have territorial[38] or personal[39] jurisdiction, and the crimes must fall within its subject matter jurisdiction: genocide, war crimes, crimes against humanity, or aggression.[40] The crimes must also have happened following the date of the entry into force by the Statute.[41] Taken together, these limitations give a view of the Court's jurisdiction as highly specialised.

The power of the ICC is derived from the Rome Statute, which binds by consent[42] the States Parties. Their ratification of the treaty evidences their acceptance[43] of the Court's jurisdiction, but it may also permit the Prosecutor to begin an investigation.[44] This power allows the Court to exercise jurisdiction in States which have not subscribed to the Rome Statute, although the same principle underpins both exercises of jurisdiction: the consent of States. The contractual agreement[45] of States gives the Court authority to act, as they

[35] The situation in Darfur, UNSC Resolution S/RES/1593 of 31 March 2005, 1 and the situation in Libya, UNSC Resolution S/RES/1970 of 26 February 2011.
[36] ibid.
[37] ibid, 2.
[38] Article 12(2)(a), Rome Statute.
[39] Article 12(2)(b), Rome Statute.
[40] Article 5, Rome Statute.
[41] Article 11(1), Rome Statute.
[42] Article 1(1)(b), Vienna Convention on the Law of Treaties 1969.
[43] Article 12(1), Rome Statute.
[44] Article 12(3), Rome Statute.
[45] Samantha Besson, 'The Authority of International Law – Lifting the State Veil' (2009) 31 Sydney LR 343.

are willing to be bound by the rules and thus subject to its jurisdiction. The subject matter jurisdiction of the Court restricts its remit to specific crimes, which must reach a certain threshold of gravity[46] before they fall within the jurisdiction of the Court. This is much more straightforward[47] than territorial jurisdiction, but a restriction on acting only in those territories which are covered by State agreement may give rise to the argument that the Court lacks authority over the commission of any crimes within its jurisdiction and therefore is limited in its authority to end impunity. The limitation, of applying only to those who have subscribed, is a clear hindrance to the Rome Statute, particularly where some of the most fragile areas of the world have not acceded to the Rome Statute.[48] Such areas would only be able to have referrals made by the UNSC but, if such a country were a State Party, the Prosecutor would only begin an investigation where there was a lack of prosecution, or possible prosecution at the domestic level.

This leads on to the next requirement, that of the State being 'unwilling or unable genuinely'[49] to prosecute those accused of the crimes at issue. The doctrine of complementarity means that the primary obligation to prosecute rests with the State, returning the authority to the State as the key legal power in terms of the prosecution of such offences. An investigation into a situation would only commence should the State satisfy the 'unwilling or unable' test, which would allow the Court to proceed should there be unjustified delays in investigating or prosecuting within the domestic system[50] or an attempt to protect an indicted person from prosecution by domestic courts.[51] This 'complementary'[52] element to the ICC's jurisdiction adds a further layer to the Court's admissibility threshold; there ought to be a reasonable possibility of prosecution by domestic authorities and should this not be the case, the Court may proceed.[53]

46 Article 17(1)(d), Rome Statute; *see* M El-Zeidy, 'The Gravity Threshold under the Statute of the International Criminal Court' (2008) 19 CLF 35, 36, on the importance of not slowing down the Court with an 'excessive and disproportionate workload.'

47 *See* McGoldrick (n 24) 627, 628.

48 Neither Iraq nor Syria have ratified the Rome Statute, and are currently worst affected by the criminal acts of Daesh, which has caused an enormous humanitarian disaster; *see* UNSC Resolution S/RES/2258 of 22 December 2015 which speaks of the 'devastating humanitarian situation' in Syria.

49 Article 17(1)(a), Rome Statute. *See* Carsten Stahn, 'A Tale of Two Notions of Complementarity' (2008) 19 CLF 87.

50 Article 17(2)(b), Rome Statute.

51 Article 17(2)(a), Rome Statute.

52 Article 1, Rome Statute. *See also* William Schabas, 'Complementarity in Practice: Some Uncomplimentary Thoughts' (2008) 19 CLF 5.

53 See *Prosecutor v Saif Al-Islam Gaddafi and Abdullah Al-Senussi* ICC-OI/II-OI/IIOA6, 24 July 2014.

Domestic authorities must be given the opportunity to prosecute and, in the absence of compelling reasons, the Court may not attempt to exercise universal jurisdiction over any and all States. An interesting development, however, has altered the course of this idea, with the greater use of the self-referral mechanism by States[54] which seek to utilise the Court as an alternative to domestic prosecutions.[55] Although a deeper exploration of this and the reasons therefore are beyond the scope of this work, it has complicated matters where the Court's commitment to complementarity has been questioned. Gondi noted that the Court had failed to return election violence cases to national courts in Kenya and cited this as an example of its failure to respect complementarity.[56] Following this line of argument, complementarity does not always work as it should in practice.

The authority of the Court is accordingly a complex issue. The ICC does have the authority to act, which can be derived from States Parties which have signalled their intention to be bound through signature and ratification. Authority from this perspective is thus permission: the Court may exercise jurisdiction under agreement. Where States Parties, and even non-States Parties, may refer themselves to the Court, the basis for authority remains permission, reflected in the concept that non-States Parties should also consent to an investigation on their territories. However, there is a critical exception to this rule of permission, specifically where the jurisdiction of the Court has been triggered by a UNSC referral.[57] Thus, there is a connection between the priorities of the UNSC and jurisdiction, as well as permission. This could include the UNSC's opinion on the effect a situation may have on international peace and security.[58] The power of the Court to act thus goes beyond State permission, but this complicates the matter of its authority. A lessening of the authority of the ICC to a simple understanding of the permission of

[54] Article 14, Rome Statute; *see also* Robinson (n 21) 323; Steven Roper and Lillian Barria, 'State Cooperation and International Criminal Court Bargaining Influence in the Arrest and Surrender of Suspects' (2008) 21 LJIL 457.

[55] Each of the situations in Mali, the Central African Republic, and Uganda were referred by the individual governments.

[56] James Gondi, 'Debunking the Conspiracy Theory: Analysing the Failure to Achieve Complementarity and the Responsibility to Protect in Kenya and Other Jurisdictions' in Steve Ndirangu, Edigah Kavulavu and Terry Jeff Odhiambo (eds), *International Criminal Justice: The ICC and Complementarity* (ICJ Kenya 2014).

[57] Article 13(b), Rome Statute. *See also* S Papillon, 'Has the United Nations Security Council Implicitly Removed Al Bashir's Immunity?' (2010) 10 ICLR 275.

[58] The involvement of the 'international community' as a defining element of an international criminal court is discussed in Astrid Kjeldgaard-Pedersen, 'What Defines an International Criminal Court? A Critical Assessment of "the Involvement of the International Community"' (2015) 28 LJIL 113.

States or the authorisation of the UNSC could create serious problems for the legitimacy of the ICC. The role of power and its impact on the ICC ought to receive further treatment.

4.4 THE ROLE OF POWER POLITICS IN THE AUTHORITY OF ICL

The ICC was intended to mark a new dawn of justice,[59] in which justice as a value could be delivered by international law and beyond States. However, it has been argued that the creation of the ICC demonstrates the limited nature of the criticism regarding power politics, in that it does not contribute to the power of States or their strategic interests.[60] This perspective does not consider, however, the idea that most prosecutions thus far have been of nationals of African States, undermining the argument that it does not contribute to the strategic interests of certain States. Tribunals tend to be supported by liberal states who believe in legalism,[61] although such States are rarely the subject of investigations by the ICC, whether as States Parties or by referral. The ICC is supported and funded significantly by powerful states and thus power plays a significant role.[62] There is the further issue of the influence of Westernism more generally in international courts and tribunals; the International Court of Justice has been argued to have been a Western conception and the creation of major criminal tribunals has been based on the civil and common law traditions[63] without much regard for other methods of justice. Indeed, the distinctions between the International Criminal Tribunal for Rwanda and the Gacaca courts were notable: there was a key focus by the Gacaca courts on restorative justice[64] and the encouragement of confession and forgiveness.[65]

The lack of connection between the ICC and methods of transitional justice (Colombia is still under preliminary examination[66]) reflects the power politics which influence the Court. Emerging powers similarly seek to

[59] Christopher Rudolf, *Power and Principle* (Cornell University Press 2017), 3–4.

[60] ibid 5.

[61] ibid 16.

[62] ibid 58.

[63] Rob de Wijk, *Power Politics: How China and Russia Reshape the World* (Amsterdam University Press 2015), 10.

[64] Erin Daly, 'Between Punitive and Reconstructive Justice: The Gacaca Courts in Rwanda' (2001) 34 NYU J Int'l L & Pol 355.

[65] Coel Kirkby, 'Rwanda's Gacaca Courts: A Preliminary Critique' (2006) 2 JAL 94; Hollie Nyseth Brehm, Christopher Uggen and Jean-Damascène Gasanabo, 'Genocide, Justice, and Rwanda's Gacaca Courts' (2014) 30 JICJ 333.

[66] Report on Preliminary Examination Activities 2020 (Colombia) 14 December 2020, Office of the Prosecutor.

conform to international institutions, where it reflects their interest.[67] This Western dominance is viewed as limited in duration by some scholars, including de Wijk, who argues that 'Western dominance of world politics can no longer be taken for granted, and a change of course is essential in order to be able to respond to the geopolitical changes.'[68] Although possible, and potentially waning, the institutions established will not dissolve overnight and the power in place, backed by economics, undermines again any immediate or short-term change. As Krasner notes, 'the centrality of power as a concept connects ideas in international politics.'[69] The inequality, therefore, of actors predicates certain political outcomes, although it can be difficult to identify, as Finnemore and Goldstein note, both State interests and State power because of their elusive nature.[70] From a political perspective, the 'thinness' of international norms[71] means that other factors such as social norms may affect behaviour at the international level,[72] although the argued conflation between power and authority may make this difficult to identify. Lake's work notes that there is a 'poor concept' of power with too much focus on coercion rather than political authority.[73] Moreover, he does not divide authority and coercion, because of a belief that the two are intertwined,[74] and influenced, as discussed earlier, by social norms.[75]

Power and dominance, from this perspective, appears to be conducted through institutions, rather than being identifiable by acts. This reflects the point made by Scheipers which holds that international law creates an order which can be contested,[76] but that it is not an instrument of power politics.[77] Instead, there are exercises of power politics, although it is difficult to see how the creation of an order, and placing it into operation, is not an enduring

[67] de Wijk (n 63) 70.

[68] ibid 187.

[69] Martha Finnemore and Judith Goldstein, 'Power Politics in the Contemporary World: Lessons from the Scholarship of Stephen Krasner' 18–27, 26 in Martha Finnemore and Judith Goldstein (eds), *Back to Basics: State Power in a Contemporary World* (Oxford University Press 2013).

[70] ibid 18–27, 18.

[71] ibid 18–27, 24.

[72] ibid.

[73] David A Lake, 'Authority, Coercion and Power in International Relations' 55–77, 55 in Martha Finnemore and Judith Goldstein (eds), *Back to Basics: State Power in a Contemporary World* (Oxford University Press 2013).

[74] ibid 55–77, 58.

[75] ibid.

[76] Sibylle Scheipers, *Negotiating Sovereignty and Human Rights: International Society and the International Criminal Court* (Manchester University Press 2012), 4.

[77] ibid 4.

exercise of power politics. Although there are arguments, such as the judicial independence of the Court, to state that it is not an exercise of power politics, it would be naïve to disregard the influence of powerful States, which will be discussed in greater detail in the next chapter. It is possibly worth noting the irony of the statement of the US Ambassador to the ICC, who stated that international law cannot be made into what we wish it to be,[78] suggesting the existence of an anchoring authority that is frequently overlooked by powerful States. This contested order is in part due to sovereignty;[79] without legalism, power would be the defining feature of any exercise of authority,[80] undermining the quality of the authority and challenging its legitimacy.

The role of power in moving international legal authority from formal legal into de facto authority is key because of the two key components, identified by Alter, Helfer, and Madsen in their work as, firstly, the recognition of 'an obligation to comply with court rulings' and secondly, 'engaging in meaningful action pushing toward giving full effect to those rulings.'[81] They are in agreement with Peters and Schaffer, who make the point that 'legitimate authority' is tautological,[82] but develop the argument that, in practice, institutions might have authority without legitimacy.[83] Their conclusions are around the idea of authority as being non-binary but rather varied between different groups.[84]

In a further piece connected with the project, Vinjamuri notes that the ICC has stronger authority among, for example, non-governmental organisations (NGOs) than among actors.[85] She goes on to note that self-referral may also indicate an acknowledgement of the Court's authority, but may also be calculated to protect government officials.[86] Although no evidence is provided for this argument, there have been some instances, for example in Katanga,[87] where the defence alleged that the focus on armed militia detracted from prosecution of government officials who were also alleged to have carried out

78 ibid 1.
79 ibid 20.
80 ibid 27.
81 Karen J Alter, Laurence R Helfer and Mikael Rask Madsen, 'The Variable Authority of International Courts: How Context Shapes the Authority of International Courts' (2016) 79 Law Contemp Probl 1, 7.
82 ibid 1, 7.
83 ibid 1, 6.
84 ibid 1, 36.
85 Leslie Vinjamuri, 'The International Criminal Court and the Paradox of Authority', 275–288 in Karen J Alter, Laurence R. Helfer and Mikael Rask Madsen, 'The Variable Authority of International Courts: How Context Shapes the Authority of International Courts' (2016) 79 Law Contemp Probl 1.
86 ibid 1, 282.
87 *The Prosecutor v Germain Katanga* ICC-01/04-01/07.

war crimes and crimes against humanity. She also notes, following Bosco,[88] that the ICC has 'made space' for Western actors,[89] a point which is supported well by the earlier discussion of the military intervention in Libya[90] and subsequent investigation.[91] She concludes by noting that this is a problem for sovereignty and creates a pretence that justice is free from political interference.[92] These problems are critical to an understanding of the use of power at the ICC, because of its Western basis and arguable anti-African bias, both of which are rooted in an empirical understanding of the Court as an institution. Moreover, although the aim is to deliver justice, these issues obfuscate that aim and undermine its delivery because of the challenge that all actors are not treated in an equitable manner. There is a discernible tension between the enforcement of rights, the delivery of justice as a value, and the question of authoritative actions, where legitimacy is paramount. Legitimacy may be achieved by seeking to satisfy these aims, but it is difficult to achieve them within this context.

Buchanan holds that the idea of legitimacy is that the international system must protect basic human rights,[93] despite the system regularly failing to do so. However, in Alter's work, she notes that 'all legal interpretation has a political element'[94] and compulsory jurisdiction creates independence for courts.[95] International courts which promoted governmental aims can be more effective[96] although this is unproven as smaller governments are not frequently consulted regarded international affairs. As a clear example, Namibia cannot become a member of the permanent five on the UNSC. The idea here is that international courts have been weak, that states are embarrassed into compliance,[97] and that national judicial acceptance has been slow.[98] The opposite is true with the ICC, where States have keenly self-referred even where their domestic courts have prosecuted individuals within the context of the conflict investigated by the ICC. International courts 'wield neither the purse nor the

88 David Bosco, *Rough Justice* (Oxford University Press 2014).
89 Vinjamuri (n 85) 1, 287.
90 See Chapter 3.
91 Decision Assigning the Situation in the Libyan Arab Jamahiriya to Pre-Trial Chamber I ICC-01/11, 4 March 2011.
92 Vinjamuri (n 85) 1, 288.
93 Allen Buchanan, *Justice, Legitimacy, and Self-Determination: Moral Foundations for International Law* (Oxford University Press 2003), 203.
94 Karen Alter, *The European Court's Political Power* (Oxford University Press 2009), 30.
95 ibid 29.
96 ibid 44.
97 ibid 92.
98 ibid 93.

sword'[99] and with their law, the lack of compulsory jurisdiction means, according to Alter, that it encourages judges to work to please governments.[100] This may apply in the context of other courts but has not been evidenced by the work of the ICC. Indeed, the ICC seems to sit outside these conceptualisations of how courts work at the international level.

The ICC has compulsory jurisdiction at the individual level, but a degree of optional jurisdiction at the State level, where complementarity may have a greater or lesser influence depending on the situation at hand. There is also a tension between domestic courts and the ICC,[101] and there may be engagement between national and international bodies[102] particularly in cases of referral. The argument that States can enforce the law much more easily than courts[103] because they can deploy force is defeated somewhat by ICL; complementarity has a number of examples where the domestic States have been completely unable to deploy appropriate force or even to arrest suspects. When mentioning international courts, Alter lists the ICC[104] but does not note that it lacks compulsory jurisdiction. In this way, the work of the ICC, and ICL more generally, sits apart as a singular example of how the law has authority at the international level. Perhaps it represents a blend of old-style methods and new-style methods; an approach of complementarity yet a breach of sovereignty when required, in theory.

4.5 CONCLUSION

International criminal law, as traced to the Nuremberg trials, has no clear source of authority. An examination of the founding documents, and diplomatic discussions which led to the creation of the Tribunal, uncovers the link between the trials and the UN structure, particularly the duty to maintain peace and security. This nebulous duty was then the basis for the international military tribunals and has remained the basis for the exercise of such power ever since. Subsequent tribunals have also been created on the basis of Chapter VII powers, including hybrid tribunals created by agreement at the domestic level. In a similar way, the basis for the instigation of the Rome Statute, and the development of the idea of an international criminal court,

99 Karen Alter, *The New Terrain of International Courts: Courts, Politics, Rights* (Princeton University Press 2014), 4.
100 ibid 7.
101 ibid 12.
102 ibid 20.
103 ibid 32.
104 ibid 79–82.

originated in the UN's responsibility for the maintenance of peace and security. However, the Rome Statute goes beyond this power, as a separate and distinct institution at the international level. Its powers are connected to the idea of peace and security, as outlined in the UN Charter, and its authority can also be derived from the consent of its States Parties. To complicate matters further, the jurisdiction of the Court goes beyond those who have consented to its jurisdiction, to States and entities referred to the Court by other States Parties and the UNSC itself. Moreover, non-state actors may also be referred to the Court for prosecution.

This expansive form of jurisdiction means that its authority goes beyond the UN's powers to maintain peace and security, and beyond the consent of States. The difficulty of pinpointing exactly its authority is similar to that of the original military tribunals, in that there is no clear designation of its authority. Instead, there is an obligation to 'end impunity' and to ensure that the interests of justice are met. Accordingly, the authority of ICL depends heavily on the tribunal at hand and whether the individual before the Court has a jurisdictional tie to a State Party. Thus, the role of power politics is not only visible, but potentially exerts a strong influence on the Court itself and the decision to prosecute. The role of power politics in creating orders is not only visible, but a requirement: the combined necessity of the maintenance of peace and security via the UN, the understanding that a Court was required to ensure that there was a method of prosecution at the international level for atrocities, which secures legitimacy through the delivery of justice and the protection of rights. However, power and wealth allow the Court to be created, and for the establishment of an order. As demonstrated by the situations before the Court, they rarely involve States capable of contesting the authority of the ICC, or even of prosecuting at the domestic level. As such, the next chapter will explore the role of sovereignty and complementarity in the work of the Court, and how this may be affected by a lack of clearly outlined authority.

5

Sovereignty and Complementarity

5.1 INTRODUCTION

The work so far has discussed the connection between authority and legitimacy, and the way in which law seeks to claim authority. In the context of public international law, various claims for authority can rest on the ability of the State to secure rights for its polity as well as the extent to which it can deliver justice. Similarly, although there is a lack of a clear basis for authority in international criminal law, its work to provide authority anchors it to something beyond the consent of States and the role of the UN Charter. The blend of moral authority and political power appears to guide the ICC, with a focus on the delivery of justice and the protection of individual rights. This is particularly supported, and undermined, by the States Parties responsible for the drafting and signing of the Rome Statute, as well as those most responsible on the UNSC. The role of power politics in international criminal law and the ICC in particular is significant, and this effect is most clearly seen when power is wielded by powerful sovereign States. The power of such States, who are more likely to be funders of the Court, and the likelihood of such power affecting the work of the Court needs to be examined in the context of the concept of sovereignty. The issue of complementarity, as a mechanism of both protection and one which more powerful States tend not to engage with, will also be examined.

Typically, developed countries with respected and operational legal systems in the common law or civil traditions would not expect to submit to the authority of the Court because of the doctrine of complementarity. The functioning nature of their systems, as well as the evidence to demonstrate the operation of the rule of law in such States, protects them. Their sovereignty thus has greater value. This means that international criminal law has varying forms of authority, and effectively could have more over weaker, less stable States. This can be seen in entities such as the Assembly of States Parties, in which decisions can be taken regarding the amendment of the Rome Statute, and even where the permanent five members of the Security Council may authorise an investigation by the Court, without the consent or even acquiescence of weaker States. The argument that 'sovereignty costs'[1] are higher for more powerful States is questionable in international criminal law, because of the way in which power is exercised in respect of the Court. Typically, developed countries with respected and operational legal systems in the common law or civil traditions would not expect to submit to the authority of the Court because of the doctrine of complementarity. The functioning nature of their systems, as well as the evidence to demonstrate the operation of the rule of law in such States, protects them. Arguably, this affords their sovereignty greater value, while undermining the sovereignty of other States, in the pursuit of justice and the protection of rights. The corollary, of protecting individual rights and securing justice, is only possible as a value where all States are held equally responsible, either domestically or internationally. Without such accountability, international criminal law has varying forms of authority, and effectively more over weaker, less stable States.

The question of the interaction between sovereignty and complementarity is therefore critical and will be examined by this chapter. This involves an analysis, firstly, of the concepts of sovereignty and complementarity, including a discussion of the concept of 'sovereignty costs.' Examples of complementarity in action will then be explored to determine whether complementarity as a concept undermines the authority the Court has, or whether it operates to reinforce its authority. This will then be contrasted with the idea of shielding, in that certain, more powerful countries have the ability to use complementarity as a shield, preventing the prosecution of those accused of war crimes and crimes against humanity at either the domestic or international levels. This is particularly relevant in the context of the investigation by the Court in Afghanistan, and the attempts to prosecute in both the UK and Australia in respect of the crimes in Afghanistan. This leads on to the question of whether the sovereignty of more powerful States simply holds more weight than that of less powerful States. This question is particularly important for international criminal law because of the effect a steep asymmetry would have on the authority of the ICC. Although it may be recognised in other areas that the votes and vetoes of powerful States count for more at the international level, a Court which seeks to end impunity, enforce the rule of law, and provide

[1] Sibylle Scheipers, *Negotiating Sovereignty and Human Rights: International Society and the International Criminal Court* (Manchester University Press 2012), 3.

justice for victims without a need to rely on domestic systems would be particularly damaged by any such effect. An examination of the impact of both sovereignty and complementarity on the authority of the Court is thus vital.

5.2 SOVEREIGNTY AND COMPLEMENTARITY

The concept of sovereignty is, accordingly to Crawford, the 'full complement of rights and obligations' for States.[2] From the perspective of authority, it allows States jurisdiction over their own affairs and presumes political and legal authority to act both domestically and at the international level. Austin's view was that everyone in society could be sovereign[3] should they be capable of 'competence' but no such measure is afforded at the international level. In order to be sovereign, States must be recognised as States, which ultimately requires recognition by the UN,[4] rather than basic compliance with the Montevideo criteria.[5] Sovereignty is thus a sword and shield at the international level: it allows States to behave independently and protects them from external interference in their domestic affairs. As a concept in international law, it would appear fundamentally incompatible with the broad ideas of human rights and international criminal justice: a full, perhaps absolute, concept of sovereignty disregards anything more than transnational law and rejects the idea of a body such as the UNSC having the power to execute any decisions in respect of international peace and security. Absolute authority at the domestic level is compatible with absolute sovereignty, but, as has been demonstrated in the preceding text, this can vary from State to State. This makes the situation much more complex than any form of absolutism would demonstrate.

Indeed, sovereignty is often referred to as a problem which must be overcome, in pursuit of a fairer world order: institutionalisation of the rule of law is required to achieve legitimacy to constrain the rich and powerful.[6] This represents an interventionist approach, in that war crimes and crimes against humanity can only be stopped by force.[7] This can be contrasted with

2 James Crawford, *Brownlie's Principles of Public International Law* (Cambridge University Press 2017).

3 John Austin, *The Province of Jurisprudence Determined* (first published 1832, General Books 2012).

4 James Crawford, *The Creation of States in International Law* (Oxford University Press 2007).

5 Article 1, The Montevideo Convention on the Rights and Duties of States 1933.

6 Scheipers (n 1) 52.

7 ibid 63.

the idea of sovereigntism, which holds that human rights and other forms of justice are enforced more effectively within State structures.[8] Naturally, this includes the idea that States can create supranational structures, but it defaults to the notion that the State possesses primary authority to prosecute and adjudicate on matters of rights and justice; all power and authority rests with the State, ultimately. This approach is difficult to appreciate in light of the preceding discussion regarding competing authorities, and it also presumes a basic level of power that all States should have. This is not the case for every State, particularly in respect of failed States.

Robert Cryer also adopts a dual view of sovereignty, distinct from the above discussion: in his view, it is either 'pre-legal,'[9] in that it was absolute and related to a State, 'monolithic' in form,[10] powerful and indivisible. The alternate view is that international law constitutes sovereignty, not only respecting it but recognising its existence, and that it is essentially a collection of rights and obligations.[11] He references the work of Clapham in relation to human rights, noting that States which breach rights should no longer be afforded the rights associated with statehood.[12] However, it is difficult to see how this would work in practice: rich, powerful States in particular remain capable of making rules at the international level, and statehood has not been revoked from any States in light of evidence of flagrant violations of human rights and international criminal law. In the case of complementarity, the very doctrine constitutes a recognition of sovereignty: it automatically limits the power of the Court. The approach of the ICC falls somewhere between the two: the primary responsibility for prosecution is with the State, but, as Stahn notes, complementarity is required to support the international system more broadly.[13] He openly acknowledges that part of the purpose of complementarity is to 'protect or maintain' domestic prosecution,[14] thus maintaining the domestic system as the primary source of authority.

Complementarity, as a doctrine, is found under several articles in the Rome Statute, primarily that of Article 17(1) in which the ICC may intervene only where the State is 'unwilling or unable' to prosecute. In setting such a threshold, the Statute, according to Stahn, 'organises' the interaction between

8 ibid 100.

9 Robert Cryer, International Criminal Law vs State Sovereignty: Another Round? (2005) 16 EJIL 979, 981.

10 ibid 979, 981.

11 ibid 979, 982.

12 ibid.

13 Carsten Stahn, 'A Tale of Two Notions of Complementarity' (2008) 19 CLF 87.

14 ibid 87, 92.

national and international jurisdictions.[15] Complementarity has been recognised as a key doctrine which may 'regulate' the interaction of domestic and international law under the Rome Statute.[16] Delmas-Marty divides the doctrine into separate notions of inability and unwillingness, with the opening of an investigation alone not constituting the necessary 'will' to prosecute. In the context of inability, she cites the six reasons given by the ICC in the situation of Darfur which would allow it to prosecute, including the lack of a significant financial burden to the international community and the ability of the ICC to intervene immediately.[17]

Accordingly, the question of complementarity is not set in stone, but represents a blend of prosecutorial policy, resources, and the context of the situation which may be examined or investigated. The question of authority is almost absent from the discussions: it is very much, in this context, a practical issue of who can effectively prosecute, rather than who or what may have the authority to do so. Delmas-Marty's conclusion of international criminal law being a 'multipolar space'[18] is fascinating, but denies the existence of power politics, or the effect on domestic authority. In the context of Sudan, a non-State Party, the authority of the domestic court, or any form of potential hybrid tribunal was rejected in favour of an international prosecution.

As such, the assumptions around complementarity are many and varied: as a doctrine, it relies on the existence and operation of a domestic legal system. It makes several assumptions regarding domestic prosecution: funding, the existence of the rule of law, and, notably, peace. A State may be willing, but the ability to prosecute is very much predicated on their situation as an entity which, as will be discussed in later chapters, may be beyond their control. Moreover, the existence of a functioning legal system, unencumbered with many of the difficulties faced by developing countries, is not really set out by the Statute. There are other issues around the due process afforded by domestic prosecutions,[19] which is argued by Heller to be a deficiency of complementarity, in that standards of fairness are not set out by the Statute. The idea of tolerating imperfect prosecutions has been posited by other scholars[20] but these

[15] ibid 87, 91, and 101.

[16] Mireille Delmas-Marty, 'Interactions between National and International Criminal Law in the Preliminary Phase of Trial at the ICC' (2006) 4 JICJ 2, 4.

[17] ibid 2, 6.

[18] ibid 2, 11.

[19] Kevin Jon Heller, 'The Shadow Side of Complementarity: The Effect of Article 17 of the Rome Statute on National due Process' (2006) 17 CLF 255.

[20] Frédéric Mégret and Marika Giles Samson, 'Holding the Line on Complementarity in Libya: The Case for Tolerating Flawed Domestic Trials' (2013) 11 JICJ 571.

are all questions subsequent to the initial question of whether a trial is actually possible. Where a trial of sorts cannot be conducted at the national level, complementarity should usually then be triggered, in that the ICC will be empowered to act where the State is 'unable or unwilling' under Article 17. This would also be outwith circumstances in which situations were referred by the State Party, other States Parties or the UNSC itself, if the situation undermined international peace and security.

Complementarity, as a doctrine, intends to situate the authority for prosecution with the domestic system, primarily, and in doing so, recognises its sovereignty. However, this idea, this method of organisation, is replete with presumptions regarding the effectiveness of the State's sovereignty. It also raises the question of whether complementarity constitutes an automatic transfer of authority from already damaged, weakened States. This is particularly interesting where the Court maintains a 'watching brief' by way of a preliminary examination in respect of a State because of the way in which it prioritises rights and justice over State sovereignty. However, the failure to engage equitably with States, or to rely upon Western legal systems to discharge their obligations without any oversight, is problematic. The next step is to examine situations in which the doctrine of complementarity was engaged, and where the ICC has either supported or returned cases to the domestic level, under the concept of complementarity.

5.3 THE ISSUE OF POSITIVE COMPLEMENTARITY

Complementarity has thus placed a limitation on the Court itself, where it is bound to recognise the sovereignty of nation States and to allow domestic prosecution, regardless of the gravity threshold, where the State is willing and able to prosecute. The effect this has on authority is interesting, in that the domestic government is recognised to be the primary holder of rights and obligations in situations where a domestic prosecution is possible, without a generalised understanding of what trials should look like at the domestic level. There have been several investigations by the Court in which complementarity has played a role. In its annual reports on preliminary investigations, the Court highlights the way in which it interacts with domestic prosecutions and where it is continuing to investigate, as well as where arrest warrants may be launched to move from the investigation of a situation to the prosecution of a case. The extent to which the Court struggles to assert its authority against that of the domestic court varies and, interestingly, does not always relate to the degree of power possessed by the State itself. At the same time, there are few examples of situations which are being investigated by the ICC which concern powerful and rich Western States, despite the engagement of such States in several recent international conflicts. The aim of this discussion is not to examine every situation in which complementarity has played a role: this would be extensive and many situations engage complementarity in a reasonably straightforward way, without discussing the roles of power and authority (and thus contributing to the continuation of the international system as it currently exists). Rather, it is considered more constructive to analyse the way in which the Court values the use of preliminary investigations to 'stimulate genuine national proceedings' against the individuals accused of significant responsibility in the commission of war crimes and crimes against humanity.[21]

The approach of positive complementarity has gone beyond the bounds of the Rome Statute, which requires investigation and prosecution where the State is unwilling or unable and appoints the Court to a role of support and encouragement for national prosecution. In Katanga, the Court offered a definition of 'unwillingness' that went quite far in terms of reluctance, including situations of shielding an individual from prosecution and where a State, for other reasons, did not wish to exercise prosecution at the domestic level.[22] Interestingly, it is also capable of observing the national process and taking steps to prosecute where there is a degree of 'inactivity.'[23] Thus, the unwillingness of the State is intrinsically connected to the evidence of its action: as long as there is a genuine attempt at domestic prosecution, it cannot be admissible under article 17.[24] The previous argument that an unfair trial at the domestic level, or that which did not satisfy due process, would still be considered a genuine attempt to prosecute[25] has been undone to an extent where the violations of due process would be considered egregious.[26] The understanding that a trial of sorts at the domestic level would support positive complementarity is also somewhat undermined by the role of the ICC in investigating situations and maintaining a watching brief on the conduct of such trials.

[21] Office of the Prosecutor Report on Preliminary Activities, December 2011, p. 5.

[22] Judgment on the Appeal of Mr. Germain Katanga against the Oral Decision of Trial Chamber II of 12 June 2009 on the Admissibility of the Case ICC-01/04-01/07 OA 8, 25 September 2009, paras 74–79.

[23] ibid; Patricia Pinto Soares, 'Positive Complementarity and the Law Enforcement Network: Drawing Lessons from the Ad Hoc Tribunals' Completion Strategy' (2013) 46 ILR 319, 323.

[24] Astrid Reisinger Coracini, 'Amended Most Serious Crimes: A New Category of Core Crimes within the Jurisdiction but Out of the Reach of the International Criminal Court?' (2008) 21 LJIL 699, 704.

[25] Heller, 'The Shadow Side of Complementarity' (n 19) 255.

[26] *Prosecutor v Saif Al-Islam Gaddafi and Abdullah Al-Senussi* ICC-OI/II-OI/IIOA6: 24 July 2014.

Ambos makes the argument that this relates directly to the concept of *ius puniendi*, in that States 'cannot hide behind the curtain of a post-Westphalian, Grotian sovereignty concept, but must make sure that the responsible are held accountable, otherwise the international community or third States (universal jurisdiction) will have to take care of them.'[27] This connection between positive complementarity and the obligation to punish those who have committed serious crimes relates strongly to the idea that the obligation arises from more than just the law and possibly more than morality. Ambos goes on to note the multifaceted nature of the *ius puniendi*, rooted in rights and the recognition of human dignity, citing the importance of a forum for prosecution. This approach to international criminal law justifies and substantiates a strong form of positive complementarity, supporting the notion that the Office of the Prosecutor should maintain 'watching briefs' on preliminary examinations.

One such situation is Colombia, in which the ICC opened an investigation in 2004 to monitor the domestic prosecutions under the Justice and Peace Law.[28] Since 2020, the decision was taken to conclude the preliminary examination without opening an investigation at present,[29] because of the way in which the 'evidence analysed since November 2019 indicated the Colombian authorities in general had undertaken significant steps'[30] to prosecute the crimes within the jurisdiction of the Rome Statute. In contrast, the preliminary examinations in each of Palestine, Ukraine, and Nigeria were recently concluded with proposals to request the opening of investigations into these situations. In each of these situations, the arguments that the ICC should be the court of last resort[31] and that it lacks resources to prosecute everyone[32] are very much undermined: there is a degree of primacy there for the ICC, even where there have been attempts at domestic prosecution. The glaring exception is the recent UK/Iraq preliminary examination,[33] which is one of only five

27 Kai Ambos, 'Punishment without a Sovereign? The *Ius Puniendi* Issue of International Criminal Law: A First Contribution towards a Consistent Theory of International Criminal Law' (2013) 33 OJLS 293, 314.

28 Report on Preliminary Examinations 2011, 13 December 2011, Office of the Prosecutor.

29 Report on Preliminary Examination Activities 2020 (Colombia), 14 December 2020, Office of the Prosecutor.

30 'La información analizada desde noviembre de 2019 indica que las autoridades colombianas en general han adoptado pasos significativos para abordar conductas que constituyen crímenes de la CPI, como se expresó en el Reporte Intermedio de 201242.' Report on Preliminary Examination Activities 2020 (Colombia), para 153.

31 Susana Sacouto and Katherine Cleary, 'The Katanga Complementarity Decisions: Sound Law but Flawed Policy' (2010) 23 LJIL 363, 369.

32 Soares (n 23) 319, 325.

33 Report on Preliminary Examination Activities 2020 (Colombia), 14 December 2020, Office of the Prosecutor.

examinations in the history of the Court to have been closed without further investigation. The other situations, in the Republic of Korea,[34] Gabon,[35] Honduras,[36] and the Comoros[37] failed to meet either the gravity threshold or to have crimes which fell within the subject matter jurisdiction of the Court. In the case of Honduras and Gabon, it was held that the specific attacks were not sufficient to constitute crimes against humanity and genocide, because of the number of crimes and the failure to evidence special intent in the context of genocide. In the situation relating to the Republic of Korea, the attack did not, in the opinion of the Prosecutor, meet the definition of perfidy. The situation of the Comoros, although complex,[38] related strongly to the definition of gravity as understood by the Chambers and the Office of the Prosecutor, in that it was not considered to meet the gravity threshold as required for further investigation and, ultimately, prosecution.

There is thus a distinction between these and the situation of the UK/Iraq investigation, which hinges on the idea that there has been some action taken by the authorities and therefore there is no need to pursue the case at the international level. The Prosecutor noted that the 'information available indicates that the UK authorities have not been inactive'[39] and that the Office of the Prosecutor 'cannot conclude'[40] that there had been an intention on the part of the UK authorities to shield any individuals from prosecution, despite delays and a failure to hold anyone alleged to have committed crimes to account. The restrained language in this case suggests that there may be a problem with the attempts to prosecute, but that there is simply insufficient evidence to prove these which could be relied upon in court. As Heller has noted,[41] this seems to be an incredibly high standard to which any potential investigation should be held. Moreover, it remains unclear as to

34 Situation in the Republic of Korea: Article 5 Report, June 2014, Office of the Prosecutor.

35 Prosecutor's notice of her decision under article 15(6) of the Statute, Situation in the Gabonese Republic: ICC-01/16, 11 September 2019, para 3.

36 Informe sobre las Actividades de Examen Preliminar (2015) Situaciones en Colombia y Honduras.

37 Decision on the 'Application for Judicial Review by the Government of the Comoros, Situation on the Registered vessels of the Union of The Comoros, The Hellenic Republic and the Kingdom of Cambodia ICC-01/13, 16 September 2020.

38 Kevin Jon Heller, 'The Comoros Declination – and Remarkable Footnote 20' *Opinio Juris*, 4 December 2019.

39 Situation in Iraq/UK Final Report, Office of the Prosecutor, 9 December 2020, para 275.

40 ibid, paras 498–503.

41 Kevin Jon Heller, 'The Nine Words that (Wrongly) Doomed the Iraq Investigation' *Opinio Juris*, 10 December 2020.

why prosecutorial discretion would be held to account in this way, which is beyond the requirements of the Statute. The issue of shielding is therefore worthy of further discussion.

5.4 THE PROBLEM OF SHIELDING

The issue of shielding is dealt with directly by the Statute, within article 17(2), which states:

> 'In order to determine unwillingness in a particular case, the Court shall consider, having regard to the principles of due process recognized by international law, whether one or more of the following exist, as applicable:
>
> (a) The proceedings were or are being undertaken or the national decision was made for the purpose of shielding the person concerned from criminal responsibility for crimes within the jurisdiction of the Court referred to in article 5;
> (b) There has been an unjustified delay in the proceedings which in the circumstances is inconsistent with an intent to bring the person concerned to justice;
> (c) The proceedings were not or are not being conducted independently or impartially, and they were or are being conducted in a manner which, in the circumstances, is inconsistent with an intent to bring the person concerned to justice.'[42]

The problem of shielding was anticipated by the drafters and the idea of defeating complementarity through the creation of sham trials would make the State 'unwilling' within the context of article 17(2). However, this does not always work effectively in practice. The complex nature of determining whether a State is truly unwilling where prosecutions may be ongoing is demonstrated by the preliminary examination of the situation in Iraq. In this case, the Office of the Prosecutor placed a great deal of reliance on the absence of any evidence that the British government had shielded those accused of war crimes.

The first of the ICC's preliminary examinations of British conduct during the Iraq war concluded in 2006 without proceeding to an investigation,[43] on a comparative approach to the gravity threshold.[44] The Prosecutor did note that there was a 'reasonable basis to proceed' with an investigation of the

[42] Article 17(2), Rome Statute of the International Criminal Court 1998.
[43] Letter to senders, Office of the Prosecutor, 9 February 2006.
[44] ibid 9.

allegations of wilful killing and torture, but the comparable gravity of the situation was much less than that of other situations investigated at that time, such as that of the Democratic Republic of the Congo which had a significantly higher number of alleged victims. There have been a number of legal acknowledgements of the commission of war crimes by British forces in Iraq: a court martial convicted Corporal Donald Payne of breaches of the Geneva Convention under the ICC Act in 2007,[45] with the court martial noting how difficult it had been to secure even that conviction because of the noted 'closing of ranks' by the soldiers, undermining the availability of evidence.[46] Human rights litigation ran concurrently[47] with the criminal investigations and trials, while the government launched an inquiry into whether one particular regiment in Iraq had treated detainees in a cruel and inhuman way. The Baha Mousa Inquiry[48] refused to comment on the possibility that the cruel techniques had been used beyond the regiment to avoid 'extend(ing) the scope of th(e) Inquiry disproportionately.'[49] The methods, known as the five techniques, were judged to constitute conduct just short of torture and thus 'cruel and inhuman treatment' by the European Court of Human Rights[50] when used by the British forces in Northern Ireland.

These 'breaches of discipline' were considered by the Inquiry not to be 'so widespread'[51] as to constitute a culture of violence, despite noting that these techniques were found by another government inquiry, the Compton Inquiry, in 1971.[52] Rather oddly, the report noted that the Compton report 'pleas(ed) no-one,'[53] despite the report confirming the use of the methods and affirming the cruel and inhuman nature of such treatment. It is also interesting to note here that the Secretary of State, in 1971, introduced the Compton report with the assurance that the government rejected the characterisation of the methods as having 'any element of cruelty or brutality.'[54] The historic rejection of wrongdoing by the British State is evidenced in its approach here; the United Kingdom

45 Nathan Rasiah, 'The Court Martial of Corporal Payne and Others and the Future Landscape of International Criminal Justice' (2009) 7 JICJ 177.

46 The Baha Mousa Public Inquiry Report, Volume 1, HC 1452 2011–12, 8 September 2011, 1.

47 *R. (on the Application of Mazin Mumaa Galteh Al-Skeini and Others) v The Secretary of State for Defence* [2005] EWCA Civ 1609.

48 The Baha Mousa Public Inquiry Report, Volumes 1–3, HC 1452 2011–12, 8 September 2011.

49 The Baha Mousa Public Inquiry Report, Volume 1, HC 1452 2011–12, 8 September 2011, 152.

50 *Ireland v UK* (Application no. 5310/71), 18 January 1978.

51 The Baha Mousa Public Inquiry Report, Volume 1, HC 1452 2011–12, 8 September 2011, 414.

52 ibid 1325.

53 ibid.

54 Report of the enquiry into allegations against the Security Forces of physical brutality in Northern Ireland arising out of events on the 9 August 1971, para 17.

was again, in 2011, held accountable for the torture and death of civilians in a number of separate incidents,[55] with a particularly scathing rejection of the argument by the British government lawyers that to extend jurisdiction to the area over which the British exercised control in Iraq would be tantamount to 'human rights imperialism.'[56] Judge Bonello, in his concurring opinion, stated:

> It ill behoves a State that imposed its military imperialism over another sovereign State without the frailest imprimatur from the international community, to resent the charge of having exported human rights imperialism to the vanquished enemy. It is like wearing with conceit your badge of international law banditry, but then recoiling in shock at being suspected of human rights promotion.[57]

The point remains critical in parallel: if one wishes to exercise dominance, via military imperialism or domestic trials, one must accept the obligations associated with them. Investigations did indeed begin, before the release of the Al-Skeini judgment, with the establishment of the Iraq Historic Allegations Team.[58] Despite over 1,000 allegations being made, no prosecutions were launched, and the team's work concluded in 2017.[59] Prior to its conclusion, however, another preliminary examination was re-opened by the new Prosecutor to consider, in light of new information, if there was a basis on which to open an investigation. The preliminary examination was concluded in December 2020 with an interesting conclusion: that the crimes were of sufficient gravity, that there was a reasonable basis on which to pursue the claims but that there was 'a lack of evidence on which it could rely on in court' to prove shielding.[60] The relevant paragraph states:

> After exhausting relevant lines of inquiry, the Office has not been able to substantiate, with evidence that it could rely upon in court, the allegation that decisions were taken within IHAT or the SPA to block certain lines of inquiry or that viable cases with a realistic prospect of conviction were inappropriately abandoned. While the Office cannot categorically rule out such a hypothesis, the evidence available to it at this stage does not allow it to conclude that there was intent on the part of the UK authorities to shield persons under investigation from criminal responsibility.[61]

[55] *Al-Skeini and Others v United Kingdom*, Application no. 55721/07, European Court of Human Rights, 7 July 2011.
[56] ibid, Judge Bonello concurring opinion.
[57] ibid, paras 37–38.
[58] Arabella Lang, 'Iraq Historic Allegations Team' HC Briefing Paper 7478, 22 January 2016.
[59] 'IHAT to close at the end of June' UK Ministry of Defence, 5 April 2017.
[60] Report of the Iraq Inquiry HC 264 July 2016, para 409.
[61] ibid.

Heller has analysed the decision in great detail,[62] concluding that the requirement of 'evidence that it could rely upon in court' is irrelevant, as the Prosecutor would not be required to satisfy a burden of proof where shielding was suspected. Although this is not mentioned in the Statute, there will be no investigation of the UK's conduct. This decision was met with great criticism from several quarters, including Heller's post noted above, and Human Rights Watch, which noted that 'the UK does not have a record of genuine willingness to investigate and prosecute war crimes independently.'[63] Their director, Clive Baldwin, also noted that the Prosecutor had erred in giving 'the UK government the benefit of the doubt, despite all the evidence that it is actively obstructing justice.'[64] Amnesty International were equally scathing, in their assessment that this provided 'a road-map for obstructionism.'[65] The argument regarding obstructionism is strengthened when examined in conjunction with the passage of the Overseas Operation Act through the Houses of Parliament.[66]

The purpose of the Act is to make prosecution 'exceptional'[67] in the case of service personnel and to avoid 'vexatious' civil prosecutions or actions against them.[68] Taking the judge in the court martial at his word, the issue here is not one of formal unwillingness, but rather the court's inability. The issue, prior to the reading of the Overseas Operation Bill, rested on the inability to collect sufficient evidence. A reading of these reports, the Prosecutor's final report, and the detail of the Overseas Operation Act casts a very different light on the behaviour of the UK government in respect of justice for the victims of war crimes carried out by British Army personnel. Indeed, the presumption against prosecution contained in the Act indicates that there is now a general unwillingness to prosecute. Although nothing concrete can be said about any of these points, as that is the nature of obfuscation, it is interesting to contrast this with the situation in Katanga. When the admissibility hearing rejected the challenge to admissibility made by Katanga, several points were made

62 Heller, 'The Nine Words that (Wrongly) Doomed the Iraq Investigation' (n 41).
63 Clive Baldwin, 'The ICC Prosecutor Office's Cop-Out on UK Military Crimes in Iraq' *Opinio Juris*, 18 December 2020.
64 ibid.
65 'ICC Decision on UK Military in Iraq Rewards Obstructionism' *Amnesty International* , 10 December 2020.
66 Second reading of the Overseas Operations (Service Personnel and Veterans) Bill Hansard vol 809 col 1170–1177.
67 Section 2, Overseas Operations (Service Personnel and Veterans) Act 2021.
68 Section 6(3), Overseas Operations (Service Personnel and Veterans) Act 2021.

regarding State inaction and the problems associated with prosecuting domestically. Of most interest was the question of inaction and inadmissibility.

> The proposal that 'unwillingness and inability also have to be considered in case of inaction. Such an interpretation is not only irreconcilable with the wording of the provision but is also in conflict with a purposive interpretation of the Statute. The aim of the Rome Statute is 'to put an end to impunity' and to ensure that 'the most serious crimes of concern to the international community as a whole must not go unpunished'. This object and purpose of the Statute would come to naught were the said interpretation of article 17 (1) of the Statute as proposed by the Appellant to prevail. It would result in a situation where, despite the inaction of a State, a case would be inadmissible before the Court, unless that State is unwilling or unable to open investigations. The Court would be unable to exercise its jurisdiction over a case as long as the State is theoretically willing and able to investigate and to prosecute the case, even though that State has no intention of doing so. Thus, a potentially large number of cases would not be prosecuted by domestic jurisdictions or by the ICC. Impunity would persist unchecked, and thousands of victims would be denied justice.'[69]

The British government have shown themselves to be active in the most perfunctory fashion. The Ministry of Defence has paid hundreds of thousands of pounds in compensation, instructed a set of investigations at great cost without the consequence of even one trial and only one conviction of a low-ranking, non-commissioned officer, has been obtained. The government's approach has been one of avoidance, undermining the authority of international criminal justice by placing itself beyond reproach, and painted a mask of complementary prosecutions over its failings to hold individuals to account. The question arising from such a point is whether sovereignty, consequently, counts for more in certain parts of the world.

5.5 THE VALUE OF SOVEREIGNTY

The ability of certain States to escape investigation by the ICC is interesting and leads to the constant refrain that the ICC focuses on the prosecution of African leaders and nationals of African States as the mainstay of its work. Examining the distinctions between Katanga in the Democratic Republic of Congo and the UK/Iraq leads to the conclusion that certain individuals can

[69] Judgment on the Appeal of Mr. Germain Katanga against the Oral Decision of Trial Chamber II of 12 June 2009 on the Admissibility of the Case ICC-01/04-01/07 OA 8, 25 September 2009, para 79.

shield themselves more effectively from prosecution. There are some key distinctions, in that the Democratic Republic of the Congo had referred themselves, but this is the sole distinction. As States are not in control of whether the Prosecutor begins an investigation, the question of shielding is purely one of whether the State in question is attempting to protect those accused of war crimes and crimes against humanity. The number of self-referrals by African States is no doubt higher than self-referrals from Western States, of which there are currently none, but opportunities for prosecuting Western States appear to be undertaken much less frequently. The question of shielding complicates the matter to a greater extent; it would be easy, and erroneous, to conclude that complementarity is used as a shield by powerful leaders and States, when the situation is more complicated than that.

The approach undertaken by the UK in respect of the Iraqi investigation meandered through accountability, at the international level, compensation claims which were honoured without liability, and apologies by commanding officers to the families of the victims. There is a clear recognition of wrongdoing and a failure to acknowledge the most basic precept of international criminal justice: individual criminal responsibility. Instead, the UK government has made cursory attempts at prosecution, and has given up relatively easily, citing lack of evidence as the reason for the failure to prosecute. Those attempts have included the Iraq Historic Allegations Team (IHAT), which has produced very short reports on its work, and little has been done to secure further evidence: it seems slightly conflicting that a strict and hierarchical organisation, such as the British Army, would be unable to compel any of their members to give evidence before a court. Moreover, there has been little investigation of the high command and the issuing of orders to use the five techniques, discussed earlier. The prosecution of the non-commissioned officer is as perpetrator directly, but it was not clear as to whether he had followed orders to do so. The inability to prosecute on this basis has then been echoed by the Prosecutor, who is willing to be far more flexible with the UK government than with the behaviour of other governments. Even when compliant, as in the case of the Democratic Republic of Congo, inaction and unwillingness are not connected in respect of more powerful States, while the rule seems less flexible for other States. It is deeply unhelpful to see a disparity of approaches to similar issues. As a policy in relation to more powerful States, it supports the allegations of postcolonial bias and undermines the equality of sovereign States in international criminal law.

This leads on to the question of whether the sovereignty of more powerful States simply holds more weight than that of less powerful States. This question is particularly important for international criminal law because of the effect significant asymmetry would have on the authority of the ICC.

Although it may be recognised in other areas that the votes and vetoes of powerful States count for more at the international level, a Court which seeks to end impunity, enforce the rule of law, and provide justice for victims without a need to rely on domestic systems would be particularly damaged by any such effect.

One interesting comparison is between the approach of the Colombian government and that of the UK government. Although the Colombian government have arguably had many issues with the prosecutions,[70] there are still prosecutions in progress and a stronger willingness to prosecute. In contrast, there is no longer even a willingness to prosecute in the UK and legislative attempts to block domestic war crimes prosecutions in the future. This is damaging not only to the UK's international reputation, but also to the authority of the ICC. The question of whether sovereignty counts for more in the context of Western, powerful, or rich countries is affirmed by the evidence outlined here: Colombia is to be monitored, the Democratic Republic of Congo required the assistance of the ICC, but the UK government is permitted to do as it sees fit with any prosecutions, with little recourse where there has been significant evidence of wrongdoing. There is no liability, there has been no trial, and the evidence of impunity in the case of those who have committed crimes in Iraq is enormous.

This is particularly troubling for the Afghanistan preliminary examination,[71] which is ongoing at the Court, and which focuses on the crimes committed during the military invasion in 2003 and beyond. The preliminary examination encompasses alleged crimes committed by coalition forces, including the US, the UK, and Australia. At the domestic level, there have been no prosecutions in the US in respect of Afghanistan, and there is pressure to establish an inquiry on the crimes alleged to have been committed by UK soldiers during the conflict in Afghanistan.[72] In Australia, an inquiry into war crimes committed in Afghanistan has recently concluded its work and published its report in November 2020. It focused on the alleged commission of war crimes by elite Australian soldiers in Afghanistan.[73] One of the central recommendations is around accountability, without a primary focus on legal accountability:

[70] Kai Ambos, *The Colombian Peace Process and the Principle of Complementarity at the ICC* (Springer 2010).

[71] Report on Preliminary Examination Activities 2020, 14 December 2020, Office of the Prosecutor.

[72] Rory Callinan, 'Calls for UK to Investigate Possible War Crimes in Afghanistan' *The Guardian*, 20 November 2020.

[73] Report of Inquiry under Division 4A of Part 4 of the Inspector-General of the Australian Defence Force Regulation 2016 into Questions of Unlawful Conduct Concerning the Special Operations Task Group in Afghanistan, 10 November 2020.

> While legal accountability for wrong-doing is likely to be focused on a tiny minority of personnel, there is no doubt that this goes beyond the law. Responsibility and accountability beyond purely legal matters is something that is recognised in the ADF. In 2015 Major General Sengelman quite rightly stated his intent to ensure that people should not only 'own their mistakes' but that any blame and punishment should be fairly apportioned, including acting upon any 'clear breaches of integrity or significant character flaws'. A wider organisational accountability for creating a system that made those failures possible is also required.[74]

There are significant similarities between this report and that of the Baha Mousa Inquiry, including the encouragement that many soldiers are professional and uphold the highest standards, far from committing war crimes and crimes against humanity with impunity. In both reports, there is an indication that such statements are required, despite the conflict that arises between such statements and the idea of wider cultural problems in certain aspects of the armed forces. There is also a focus in both reports on improvements for the future. Neither says much about justice for victims or whether that ought to entail prosecution, although the Australian report notes that the 'tiny minority' indicted should possibly face prosecution in civilian courts. There is little reference to the issue of justice and the idea that both countries have had powerful military presences which exercised control and violence in a way which ended the lives, in painful ways, of many ordinary civilians. The focus is very much on the institutions themselves, the broader problems with their culture, and the requirements for change. The obligations that States have in respect of rights and justice tend not to feature heavily in the reporting of such crimes; there is quite a significant gulf between the role of international criminal justice and the way in which the reports consider the idea of accountability. Although institutional change may engage accountability, there was no indication that this was the primary motivation. The values of justice and the protection of the vulnerable, of their rights, remains absent from such discussion. Although institutional change is something to be sought in the aftermath of war crimes and crimes against humanity, this is not an issue of transitional justice or the recreation of State entities. These allegations concern enormously powerful actors backed by the wealthiest, most powerful States on the planet. To avoid the mention of rights and justice in such a context is significant and speaks volumes about the priorities of such States. Those who would otherwise be affected by future crimes will be grateful for institutional change; the existing victims deserve better.

[74] ibid, para 71.

5.6 CONCLUSION

The authority of international criminal law at the ICC is reliant on its continued focus on prosecuting the most serious crimes of concern to humanity. It is acknowledged that international criminal law exists outwith the ICC, but there is no more visible and more active court in the sphere. Its permanent nature makes it the central arena in which international criminal law operates, for now. Without the recourse to grandiose language, this must mean that the ICC focuses on the most damaging cases and most concerning situations. Under article 17, that remit is extended to situations in which a domestic prosecution is unlikely for reasons of unwillingness or inability. The rejection of the prosecutor to begin an investigation into Iraq is deeply troubling, because of the precedent it sets. The UK government have successfully obfuscated and paid their way out of justice in Iraq, which is still significantly damaged almost two decades after the beginning of the war. Thus, the victims of war crimes and crimes against humanity have little recourse against the British government for any crimes committed; instead, there have been payments of compensation and apologies without formal acceptance of liability.

The authority of international criminal law rests on the precept that those who commit terrible crimes, particularly against civilians, are held to account. The way in which they are held to account predicates the existence of that authority; whether the international system can be said to be fair and apply to all, with a distinct reasoning that such justice should apply to all, or whether a privileged set of wealthy States should be able to indicate assurances that they are investigating and prosecuting, while obstructing and dampening down any threat of international humiliation. The focus of such States thus far, to use the UK government as an example, has been to prevent the indictment of any soldiers before the tribunal. The ICC, for its part, does not wish to indict British soldiers if the domestic courts can deal with the prosecution. The problem is that they cannot, and the impunity gap noted in the Democratic Republic of Congo exists in the UK as well. The crimes committed by the British forces, as attested in the trial of Donald Payne, note the disregard for life, the humiliation sought by those who committed them, and the inhuman treatment of prisoners. Such conduct was not carried out in the shadows; the evidence indicated that there were witnesses to the conduct and that it was committed openly. With evidence to support the conclusion that those who acted did so with impunity, there is a direct conflict with the UK's approach and the idea of international criminal justice. There is every indication that these are the sorts of trials in which the ICC should intervene when required.

The question of evidence and the practicality of acquiring sufficient evidence is grave, but it is difficult to argue that the Prosecutor would struggle where successful prosecutions have been launched in more difficult terrain, geographically and politically, than in the UK and Iraq. The volume of allegations could be investigated by the Court, relying on the Iraqi people to provide witness testimony. This has been possible in other trials, but the potential for reliance erodes slowly, like the shoreline, over time. As time wears on, the likelihood of prosecution ebbs, and with it the hope of justice for these victims.

It is inexplicable that the ICC should monitor some States and ignore others. The authority of the ICC requires a measured, balanced approach, particularly towards powerful States. At present, there is clear lack of balance: much more trust is imbued in the States which have power, wealth, influence. The UK approach to Iraq provides a useful roadmap for the Australian government, if they wish to follow suit. Such an approach would defeat the Court's authority and add substance to the argument that it is a tool of postcolonial oppression. The allegations of anti-African bias appear to have a stronger basis when there is a lack of prosecution at both the national and international level for Western States, particularly in the case of the UK as a State Party. Considering this, the next chapter investigates the arguments made in relation to the neo-colonial charges levelled at the Court. The question of whether the Court is truly biased is examined, to determine the impact this has, or would have, on the Court's authority.

6

Postcolonialism and Bias in International Criminal Law

6.1 INTRODUCTION

The notion of the ICC as a vehicle for neo-colonial intentions is not immediately apparent, particularly among those who support the aims of the Court. On the twentieth anniversary of the signing of the Rome Statute of the ICC, Kenneth Roth, Head of Human Rights Watch, noted the importance of the Court as part of a wider 'call for justice.'[1] The French government also emphasised the value of its budgetary commitments to the Court[2] and highlighted the importance of its endurance as a vehicle for justice. The German ambassador to the UN underscored the German government's commitment to the 'rules-based order' of which the ICC is part, stating that 'any attempt to undermine the Court should not be tolerated.'[3] Although it is not particularly surprising that those who advocate for human rights, or those who pay for the Court, would also be supportive of its aims, their words contrast sharply with the perspectives of those who find themselves in the crosshairs of the Court. President Rodrigo Duterte of the Philippines stated, at a press conference, that he would 'arrest' the Court or its representatives because of their lack of authority in the Philippines.[4] Similarly, when the ICC released a warrant for the arrest of current Sudanese President Omar al-Bashir in 2009, in respect of crimes against humanity, al-Bashir's own response was that the ICC could

[1] 'Kenneth Roth's Statement at the Commemoration of the 20th Anniversary of the Adoption of the Rome Statute of the International Criminal Court' *Human Rights Watch*, 17 July 2018.

[2] 'ICC – 20th Anniversary of the Rome Statute' *France Diplomacy*, 17 July 2018.

[3] Statement by Ambassador Christoph Heusgen on behalf of 74 States Parties to the Rome Statute in support of the International Criminal Court on the occasion of the ICC Report to the General Assembly, 2 November 2020.

[4] President Duterte, speaking about the Filipino Government's decision to withdraw from the Rome Statute, quoted in 'Duterte Threatens to Arrest International Criminal Court Prosecutor' *The Guardian*, 13 April 2018.

'eat' the warrant.[5] At the same time, the French and British Foreign Offices welcomed the decision to release the warrant, without much reference to the British colonial involvement in Sudan. This could be explained very simply: countries behave differently when subject to the jurisdiction of the Court rather than when they fund or engage with it as an exercise of power. This is particularly apparent in situations where the countries are former colonisers of the States who are subject to the Court's examinations or investigations.

However, the idea that those who exercise power through funding and supporting the Court would also be subject to the exercise of its jurisdiction is controversial. The most significant donors to the Court are Western European States, with the EU en bloc providing the majority of the funding for the ICC. Almost all the wealthiest EU Member States (and one former member) collectively colonised large parts of the African continent. These same States, which are within a century of claiming independence from their colonisers, are then subject to investigations by the Court. As of 2022, nine investigations leading to prosecutions by the Court have taken place. Of those nine, all of the States concerned were former colonies of either France, the UK, Germany, or Italy. Moreover, all the Court's successful prosecutions thus far have all been of Black African men who have taken part in armed atrocities across the continent. No Heads of State have been prosecuted successfully as of 2022. The idea of the Court focusing solely on Africans as defendants has been robustly rejected by the current Prosecutor, Fatou Bensouda:

> With due respect, what offends me most when I hear criticisms about the so-called African bias is how quick we are to focus on the words and propaganda of a few powerful, influential individuals and to forget about the millions of anonymous people that suffer from these crimes ... because all the victims are African victims. Indeed, the greatest affront to victims of these brutal and unimaginable crimes ... women and young girls raped, families brutalised, robbed of everything, entire communities terrorised and shattered ... is to see those powerful individuals responsible for their sufferings trying to portray themselves as the victims of a pro-western, anti-African court.[6]

However, the fact remains that the ICC is funded by rich, Western States who rarely find themselves under scrutiny by the Court despite participation in questionable conflicts which have resulted in the commission of war crimes, as discussed earlier. This chapter undertakes the challenge confronted by

5 'Sudanese President tells International Criminal Court to "Eat the Arrest Warrant"' *The Guardian*, 4 March 2009.

6 David Smith, 'New Chief Prosecutor Defends International Criminal Court' *The Guardian*, 23 May 2012.

Bensouda when attempting to underscore the Court's authority: the charge of anti-African bias and the argument that the Court remains a tool of postcolonialism. The economic and powerful advantages of Western States give the impression of greater control over international criminal law via the Court than would be appropriate for such a significant form of international law, potentially creating an imbalance of power.

Following on from the previous chapter, in which the issue of international criminal law having a greater degree of authority over weaker, less stable States, was explored, this chapter examines the extent to which international criminal law undermines its own authority by undertaking a postcolonial approach to the question. The discussion begins with a postcolonial approach to the question of sovereignty, strengthening the previous discussion of the value of sovereignty by examining the idea through a postcolonial lens. The question of bias at the Court will also be addressed, drawing on the literature which discusses the question of anti-African bias in the Court's approach to postcolonial States and prosecutions at the international level. The discussion will then examine the question of whether greater efforts at complementarity should be made in situations regarding African States. The Court has generally undertaken preliminary examinations in situations of self-referral or where the Prosecutor has begun an investigation on its own initiative. The extent to which other approaches to positive complementarity, such as active support for domestic prosecution, will also be discussed as a means of building capacity at the domestic level. As part of this discussion, a more general and broader approach to positive complementarity will also be discussed.

6.2 A POSTCOLONIAL UNDERSTANDING OF SOVEREIGNTY

Where colonies may have attempted to break free from colonial rule, both the international system and colonial rule decreed their inability for self-government. There is a stark contrast in approach towards emerging States in Europe and those in Africa, the former of which were afforded great opportunities to self-govern, while the latter were considered incapable of self-government. Instead, the European powers decreed that they were bound by the 'sacred trust of civilisation'[7] to maintain control over colonies.

However, the notion of sovereign equality is deeply flawed, yet has an enduring effect on the system. Nesiah holds that 'the state is perhaps the supreme icon of postcolonial modernity,'[8] while acknowledging that landscapes can't be reduced to mere territory, but rather they become 'constitutive

7 Article 22, Treaty of Versailles.

8 Vasuki Nesiah, 'Placing International Law: White Spaces on a Map' (2003) 16 LJIL 1, 2.

of the heterogenous voices that define conceptions of the nation.'[9] Nationhood, however, has been relegated in international law, replaced by statehood as the defining characteristic of those who exercise power on the international stage. As part of this, as Brolmann highlights, nationality became key. Its emergence can be traced to the rise of nation statehood in Italy and Germany, with connected protections created for those in the minority linked to a majority population elsewhere.[10] This development was contemporaneous with the development of 'distinctly artificial' borders and states in Africa, which Mutua notes as an 'interruption' of the natural evolution of political conditions in Africa. Consequently, colonial nations continued to try to aspire to the new system imposed on them; to 'develop.' This development is problematic because of its unnaturalness, and he notes that it has not worked frequently.[11] Decolonisation, he argues, 'decolonised the colonial state, not the African peoples subject to it.'[12] Self-determination therefore was exercised by the West, not those who were subject to it.

This inconsistent approach to internationalism, dependent entirely on one's geographical position, was illustrated in the previous part to this work and can be seen throughout the development of the ideas of sovereignty and statehood: Mill put forward the idea that the Native Americans lacked the capacity for self-government,[13] disregarding the established understanding of sovereignty, credited to Salvius Julianus, as being derived from the will of the people.[14] Instead, the system continued to focus on the fiction that certain States in existence cannot be 'fully . . . members of (the) family' of nations 'because their civilisation, if any, does not enable them and their subjects to act in conformity with the principles of international law.'[15] He characterises mandate or colonised States as under the protection of European States and suggests that the postcolonial position as protectorate prevents them from exercising any political influence.[16]

9 ibid 1, 35.
10 Kiki Brolmann, 'The PCIJ and International Rights of Group and Individuals' in Christian J Tams and Malgosia Fitzmaurice (eds), *Legacies of the Permanent Court of International Justice* (Martinus Nijhoff 2013), 124.
11 Makau wa Mutua, 'Why Redraw the Map of Africa: A Moral and Legal Inquiry' (1995) 16 MJIL 1113, 1115.
12 ibid 1113, 1116
13 Kanishka Jayasuriya, *Reconstituting the Global Liberal Order: Legitimacy, Regulation and Security* (Routledge 2005) 25.
14 Jill D Harries, 'Resolving Disputes: The Frontiers of Law in Late Antiquity' 68–82 in Ralph W Mathisen (ed), *Law, Society, and Authority in Late Antiquity* (Oxford University Press 2001), 71.
15 Lassa Oppenheim, *International Law: A Treatise – vol 2: Peace* (2nd edn, Longman 1912), 116.
16 ibid 147.

Oppenheim offered the example of France colonising Madagascar in 1896, as a good example of a people which 'relied' on France's support for anything they may need.[17] Indeed, according to Oppenheim, protection is the first step to annexation. However, he did say that it could be possible for the protected entity to 'shake off by force' the protectorate, with the situation of Abyssinia rejecting Italian control and colonisation being cited with approval. His complete disregard for the ability of non-European states to offer examples of sovereignty or even self-determination was not even countenanced. Colonies were to be considered 'territories of the motherland' and so the Commonwealth, under the Law of Nations, was entirely British.[18]

However, the development of the idea of sovereignty is not unknown to international jurists, including Oppenheim: He notes the introduction of the term 'sovereignty' into political science by Bodin in 'De la république' in 1577.[19] Previously, the term sovereign meant the highest power, be it political or legal. Bodin identified sovereignty as the 'highest form of power' and noted that it cannot be constitutionally limited, but only limited by the law of nature, without defining it as anything in particular. Oppenheim uses this idea of sovereignty to develop a set of conditions which should be met before statehood is achieved. These include the existence of a people, a country, a government relating to one or more persons who represent the people and are bound by the rule of law. He explicitly excludes anarchy. A sovereign government should also be present, exercising independent and supreme authority.[20] It is extremely difficult to accept that other countries, non-Western and, more often than not, non-Christian, could not meet a version of these conditions. Indeed, Anghie argues that sovereignty was improvised out of the 'colonial encounter'[21] and that the obsession with Westphalian states underlines the idea that there is too great a focus on Western identity. He mentions Vitoria and states that he noted the Spanish entitlement to a 'friendly hearing' without saying why they should be entitled to such.[22] However, I would contest the notion, based on the points made here, that sovereignty is an improvised concept. Rather, the view taken here is that sovereignty is a concept which has been applied selectively to certain States to benefit the existing power structure.

[17] ibid 147.
[18] ibid 231.
[19] ibid 67.
[20] ibid 108–109.
[21] Antony Anghie, *Imperialism, Sovereignty and the Making of International Law* (Cambridge University Press 2005), 6.
[22] ibid 23.

The selective application of the rules has privileged Western and Christian states as a means of maintaining power, not of creating a rule of law to which everyone adheres. This is particularly problematic in the sphere of international criminal justice, where the focus from a participation- and jurisdiction-based perspective is on States, who create the rules around its application. Anghie argues along similar lines, but more forcefully: he puts forward the idea that international law conceals colonialism and undermines any attempt at reparation.[23] Koskenniemi makes similar points, noting that sovereignty is always underpinned by an ideology which justifies it, but that it can only been seen when the positive rules which support or obscure it are removed.[24] In his view, the ideology was 'civilisation' which permitted the exploitation of African natural resources and the people within the colonised territories. This approach undermined any 'sovereignty' non-Western nations may have had, returning to the same logic as John Stuart Mill, who felt that India and the Indians 'required' colonisation because of their lack of capacity.[25]

Analyses of older texts demonstrate a consistency in approach to non-Western nations. Anghie's reading of Vattel also notes that the Native Americans were unable to wage a just war because they lacked a recognisable sovereign.[26] Sovereignty was therefore a specific set of practices, or a specific way of doing things, which disempowered any and all non-Europeans.[27] He makes this point again, where the treaties with non-European states were made, but unless the criteria were met they continued to lack sovereignty.[28] As part of this, positivism has dominated international law, as supported by Oppenheim. The divination of law from the behaviour of states and institutions is problematic,[29] because it reinforces these power asymmetries. Work in the area rarely challenges this understanding of treaties and their connected institutions, with recent work noting that the system established at Versailles was the beginning of our reliance on institutions for support.[30] Given the process of decolonisation began in the decades following Versailles, there is little evidence that a process of decolonisation has reached international

23 ibid 2.

24 Martti Koskenniemi, 'International Law and Empire, Aspects and Approaches' 1–20 in Martti Koskinniemi, Walter Rech and Manuel Jiminez Fonseca, *International Law and Empire* (Cambridge University Press 2017), 10.

25 Jayasuriya (n 13) 25.

26 Anghie (n 21) 26.

27 ibid 37.

28 ibid 58.

29 ibid 43.

30 Manfred Boemeke, Gerald Feldman and Elisabeth Glaser (eds), *The Treaty of Versailles: A Reassessment after 75 Years* (Cambridge University Press 1998).

institutions as well. This is particularly problematic for the authority of the ICC because of the way in which it has been created by sovereign States and is considered to have a bias against non-Western States. The ways of enforcing international criminal justice can appear Euro centric and focused on the failings of non-Western States, rather than the abuse of power by whoever may commit it.

The international law position of treaties and institutions as ways of making meaningful, enduring, and genuinely international law is flawed: the acceptance of such methods to make decisions undermines the sovereignty of certain nations, because it requires a Western conception of sovereignty, and one which does not necessarily pay much attention to the will of peoples, preferring States. As noted earlier, nationhood has been subsumed in favour of statehood, to concentrate power in the hands of those who conformed to the post-Westphalian model of governance. Arguably, there is a lack of self-reflection through the constant recourse to institutions in international law, and one which creates significant problems for postcolonial States. It is not just the way in which they are constituted, but rather the settled nature of Western States, and the absence of any significant conflict for several decades on their home soil. Power has protected such States, making situations such as September 11 the exception rather than a common occurrence. States which have experienced war, violence, and instability on a systemic basis have few opportunities to develop and acquire power in a meaningful way. The impact of colonisation, the power struggles which have followed colonisation, and the ethnic tensions which remained long after they were exploited by the colonisers[31] have an enduring impact on such States.

Such effects continue to have ramifications in these States. Because of this, the allegation that the Court focuses too much on Africa, acting in favour and rarely against Western States, is a charge which should be interrogated. The question of anti-African bias has been the subject of widespread discussion, both general[32] and in greater depth,[33] as well as the enduring question of how to ensure justice for victims on a continent scarred by instability and war. The issue of anti-African bias is particularly relevant because it presents a

[31] Marc Lacey, 'A Decade after Massacres, Rwanda Outlaws Ethnicity' *The New York Times*, 9 April 2004, www.nytimes.com/2004/04/09/world/a-decade-after-massacres-rwanda-outlaws-ethnicity.html.

[32] 'ICC debate: Africa vs "Infamous Caucasian Court"?' Al-*Jazeera*, 28 October 2016, www.aljazeera.com/news/2016/10/28/icc-debate-africa-vs-infamous-caucasian-court.

[33] W Chadwick Austin and Michael Thieme, 'Is the International Criminal Court Anti-African?' (2016) 28 Peace Review 342, 348; Oumar Ba, 'International Justice and the Postcolonial Condition' (2017) 63 Africa Today 45, discussed below.

significant challenge to the authority of the Court, in that there can be no legitimate exercise of power in international criminal justice where that power is used to continue a system of oppression. As such, any evidence of bias would create a strong challenge to the Court's authority.

6.3 THE QUESTION OF ANTI-AFRICAN BIAS

The argument that the ICC is biased against African States is borne out very clearly by a simple reading of the numbers.[34] As of 2022, there are seventeen current investigations by the Court. Eleven of these are African States, all of which are former colonies of Western European States. The preliminary examinations, as of 2022, in ten different States in total, are a little more balanced, with three focused on situations concerning African States. However, the prosecutions to date have all been of African defendants, which makes it very difficult to argue that the Court is not focused on one continent. The first Prosecutor of the Court had focused on a number of African cases, including the infamous Kenyatta case,[35] an approach considered necessary because of the lack of judicial accountability and the failure to prevent atrocities in a number of African States.[36] In his noted article on the problems with African perceptions of the Court, Jalloh quotes President Kagame of Rwanda stating that Rwanda will never be a State Party because, 'as long as you are poor, weak there is always some rope to hang you. ICC is made for Africans and poor countries.'[37] This perception, although perhaps not rooted fully in evidence, holds much sway within the African Union. Writing in 2009, Jalloh discussed the conflicts which were then under scrutiny by the Court[38] and noted the criticisms of the Court by the African Union, urging the Court to take them more seriously.[39] The idea that African countries are targeted by the Court is not a minority perspective, although the self-referrals to the Court by African States depict a complicated reality. Interestingly, much has happened since then, and the central problems are possibly less connected to African acceptance of the Court and more to the Court's approach to Western and African States. The Court's approach to African

[34] John Dugard, 'Palestine and the International Criminal Court: Institutional Failure or Bias' (2013) 11 JICJ 563, 569.
[35] James Verini, 'The Prosecutor and the President' *New York Times Magazine*, 22 June 2016.
[36] Austin and Thieme (n 33) 342, 348.
[37] Charles Chernor Jalloh, 'Regionalizing International Criminal Law' (2009) 9 ICLR 445.
[38] ibid 445, 445.
[39] ibid 445, 451.

States, beyond the acceptance of its legitimacy and its work as a legitimate exercise of power, is distinct from how they approach it.

Thus, the historical, postcolonial dimension cannot be overlooked. The use of tribunals can be viewed as selective, confirming the way in which international law still 'consecrates the West as the sole trustee of law, justice, and morality'[40] by favouring an approach to justice that follows a Western tradition.[41] This links to the idea that international law has a problem with its history; the efforts it makes to liberate itself from this and focus on fairness, morality, and justice are undermined by its colonial past.[42] The shadow imperialism casts over international criminal law and the ICC in particular undermines its legitimacy.[43] A clear-eyed view of the history of international humanitarian law has only recently been the focus of scholarly endeavours. Recent contributions note, among other things, the sad reality that Henri Dunant was a coloniser himself,[44] despite having made an enormous contribution to international humanitarian law. This amply demonstrates the way in which a legal realist approach is undermined by a failure to acknowledge the influence and role of colonialism.[45] Although postcolonialism is frequently cited by works on international criminal justice, including international humanitarian law, there are not many studies which discuss the ideas in depth. None of the major works on the Court discuss postcolonialism[46] and many others mention postcolonialism as an issue, rather than a dimension to the Court's work.[47] It is difficult to understand how the Court's authority can be properly assessed when this critical aspect of its work is so frequently

40 Ba (n 33) 45, 58.

41 HansPeter Kaul, 'The Nuremberg Legacy and the International Criminal Court: Lecture in Honor of Whitney R. Harris, former Nuremberg Prosecutor' (2013) 12 WUGSLR 637.

42 Asad G Kiyani, 'The Three Dimensions of Selectivity in International Criminal Law' (2017) 15 JICJ 624, 627.

43 Frederick Cowell, 'Inherent Imperialism: Understanding the Legal Roots of Anti-Imperialist Criticism of the International Criminal Court' (2017) 15 JICJ 667, 686.

44 Frédéric Mégrét, 'From "Savages" to "Unlawful Combatants": A Postcolonial Look at International Humanitarian Law's "Other"' 265–317 in Anne Orford (ed), *International Law and Its Others* (Cambridge University Press 2006), 308.

45 Kamari Maxine Clarke, 'Refiguring the Perpetrator: Culpability, History and International Criminal Law's Impunity Gap' (2015) 19 IJHR 592.

46 Otto Triffterer (ed), *Commentary on the Rome Statute of the International Criminal Court* (Beck Hart Nomos 2008); Roy Lee (ed), *The International Criminal Court: The Making of the Rome Statute* (Kluwer Law International 1999); Ilias Bantekas, *International Criminal Law* (Hart 2010); William Schabas, *The International Criminal Court: A Commentary on the Rome Statute* (Oxford University Press 2010); William Schabas, *The Cambridge Companion to International Criminal Law* (Cambridge 2015); Antonio Cassese, Guido G Acquaviva and Mary De Ming Fan, *International Criminal Law: Cases and Commentary* (Oxford 2011).

47 Robert Cryer, *Prosecuting International Crimes* (Cambridge University Press 2005).

relegated to the footnotes. The school of thought known as Third World Approaches to International Law offers a different path through this problem.

Third World Approaches to International Law (TWAIL) offer some perspectives on the ideas, demonstrating the importance of colonialism to the development of international law.[48] As a school of thought, it can support better approaches to justice[49] through prioritising local remedies and domestic prosecutions. The Hague's argued hegemony as the centre of justice[50] is considered problematic because it removes justice from the local area and transports it back to Europe, echoing an approach of Euro- or Western-centrism.[51] There is also a general suspicion of international law, justifiably so[52] given the previous approach of colonisers who disregarded domestic legal systems in favour of imposing those familiar to them. The fear that Africa would be a laboratory for the ICC[53] is accidentally proven by Hault's work, when he concludes that the survival of the ICC depended on African cases[54] and that its track record has provided a wealth of knowledge, improving the rule of law and the protection of human rights.[55] It is not argued that the intention was to do so by either the Court or the funders, but instead there appears to be a sort of thoughtlessness which operates in the policies undertaken by the Office of the Prosecutor (OTP) at that time. The same thoughtlessness would be difficult to countenance with more powerful States, and therefore it is not argued that it is entirely innocent, but rather an approach which disregards the equality of States. A carefully considered approach is required to avoid undermining the authority of international criminal justice to aim for justice in this way, while appreciating the way in which African cases have supported the development of the Court.

Consequently, there is a degree of suspicion around the exercise of prosecutorial discretion, as one of the main conduits for the authority of the Court. The critical element is impartiality; any evidence of politicisation, particularly

48 Jalloh (n 37) 445.

49 Antony Anghie and BS Chimni, 'Third World Approaches to International Law and Individual Responsibility in Internal Conflict' (2004) 36 Stud Transnat'l Legal Pol'y 185.

50 John Reynolds and Sujith Xavier, 'The Dark Corners of the World' (2016) 14 JICJ 959, 982.

51 Salvatore Caserta, 'Western Centrism, Contemporary International Law, and International Courts' (2021) 34 LJIL 1.

52 Asad G Kiyani, 'Third World Approaches to International Criminal Law' (2016) 109 AJIL Unbound 255, 258.

53 Kerstin Bree Carlson, *The Justice Laboratory: International Criminal Justice in Africa* (Brookings Institute 2020).

54 Derrick M Nault, *Africa and the Shaping of International Human Rights* (Oxford University Press 2020), 159.

55 ibid 160.

where it is possible to refer neighbouring States to the Court, can be problematic.[56] Such politicisation was harnessed well by the cases in Kenya: Helfer and Showalter argue strongly that the backlash against the Court generated by those indicted in the Kenyan cases undermined their prosecution.[57] Moreover, certain powerful actors who were accused of significant crimes had an interest in supporting the backlash against the Court,[58] in a bid to avoid prosecution at both the domestic and international levels. They characterised the backlash not just as a response, but as a strategy. The point made by Bensouda supports this approach; that the Court targets those in Africa who abuse power, for the benefit of African victims who would otherwise lack access to justice. Helfer and Showalter stated:

> The success of Kenya's integrated backlash strategy – as indicated in the dismissal of the prosecutions and the reduction in public and government support for the ICC across Africa – offer a troubling roadmap for other states to oppose prosecutions before the ICC as well as ad hoc or hybrid criminal tribunals. By manipulating ambiguous doctrines, challenging the legal basis for prosecutions using geopolitical arguments that appeal to neighbouring countries and by tacitly refusing to cooperate with ongoing proceedings while publicly (but disingenuously) professing to recognize the authority of the court, its judges and staff, opponents of international justice can obfuscate and delay proceedings until the prosecution is forced to make a *sua sponte* decision to dismiss the indictments.[59]

It is a relevant argument, but it dismisses too easily the problems generated by the postcolonial context, reparations for which are still due. Instead of considering how easily postcolonialism impacts the acts of the Court, it dismisses legitimate concerns without exploring how this might be dealt with by the Court. These concerns can then be harnessed easily by those seeking to evade justice on the grounds of an illegitimate prosecution, rather than genuine innocence. These fears have a solid historical basis and should be confronted squarely to ensure that the authority of the Court is not impugned when it is needed most to dispense justice. This is particularly important where the gravity threshold is considered by the Prosecutor during a preliminary exam-

[56] Alana Tiemessen, 'The International Criminal Court and the Politics of Prosecutions (2014) 18 IJHR 444.

[57] Laurence R Helfer and Anne E Showalter, 'Opposing International Justice: Kenya's Integrated Backlash Strategy against the ICC' (2017) 17 ICLR 1, 1.

[58] ibid 1, 41.

[59] ibid 1, 46.

ination. A good example of where the gravity threshold ought to have been applied clearly and effectively by the Prosecutor concerns the investigation in the Democratic Republic of the Congo. In this investigation, for example, the focus was on the conscription of child soldiers rather than the violence the accused were considered to have been responsible for. Moreover, the individuals indicted did not occupy significant leadership positions.[60] There was no significant discussion or justification for doing so, and limited discussion of the gravity threshold. Instead, the focus remained on the indicted individuals. Interestingly, the Democratic Republic of the Congo was also considered, as discussed earlier, to have met the gravity threshold in part because of the number of crimes committed, in contrast with the situation in Iraq,[61] where the number of crimes was not considered significant because they lacked sufficient gravity.

The idea that gravity could be based not on the character of the crimes but the volume of victims, is problematic, and deeply so where the State in question, in which more serious crimes are going unpunished, is African. Ba cogently expresses this idea, in that superpowers can act with impunity and affect the international legal order, without the force of the law which is used against African States.[62] The argument here is for a degree of equity in prosecution, not for the force of the law to be removed entirely. There must be a better approach, therefore, which confronts the damage done by colonialism and yet ensures that there are prosecutions, either domestically or internationally, for those who have committed such serious crimes across the board. This would preclude focus on a select number of States, and guarantee the provision of justice for victims. The focus on justice as a measure by which the Court's authority can be taken would confirm that it is not a tool of the West. It could then be argued that its legitimacy lies in its ability to dispense justice for victims where they would otherwise have none. Moreover, the location of such victims should not matter. This engages critically the question of complementarity and raises the next question, of whether complementarity can go further than it does at present, focusing on ideas that go beyond restricting prosecutions to The Hague. Moreover, the question of authority needs to be addressed through greater engagement with the domestic populations, with the victims, and with justice which is seen to be done.

60 Tiemessen (n 56) 444.
61 Letter to senders, Office of the Prosecutor 9 February 2006, 9.
62 Ba (n 33) 45, 57.

6.4 SHOULD THERE BE GREATER EFFORTS AT COMPLEMENTARITY AS AN EXERCISE OF AUTHORITY?

The concept of complementarity, as discussed earlier, notes the importance of supporting domestic trials. As noted by Heller,[63] there is no requirement set out in article 17 for a certain type of trial, or a certain standard by which trials must comply; as Mégrét and Samson note, it is simply the idea that the proceedings are genuine which matters to the Court.[64] Their argument, developing Heller's point, is that complementarity should be used in all possible situations; a bold proposition which acknowledges that human rights norms may not be respected during such trials.[65] In their view, this has the purpose of ensuring that domestic trials are prioritised over international prosecutions. Among other points, they note the importance of local trials:

> There is an inherent value in local trials, particularly in a transitional context, which is the natural counterpoint to an assertion of international jurisdiction. Local trials maximize deterrence, encourage a sense of ownership about transitional justice, and greatly facilitate the administration of justice. Such value is immensely diluted when trials are held in international fora and according to largely foreign rituals. Whatever positive message about the rule of law or due process may be communicated by The Hague is likely to be lost in translation, as populations quickly turn off from the spectacle of international criminal justice far removed from local realities.[66]

This approach undertakes a strict textual interpretation of article 17, in which the domestic prosecution is not investigated or held to specific international standards, rejecting the notion that there is a threshold below which the ICC's policy should not descend. While it might be valuable to have a certain standard, and trials which conform to international human rights, it is also, as they correctly state, not the purpose of article 17 to investigate the sort of trial which is being instigated at the domestic level. The threshold of unwilling or unable does not require an interrogation of the domestic legal system dispensing justice. Thieme and Austin make the point that this approach could be supported by African States, who could 'limit the involvement of the ICC' by focusing on the strengthening and development of domestic

[63] Kevin Jon Heller, 'The Shadow Side of Complementarity: The Effect of Article 17 of the Rome Statute on National due Process' (2006) 17 CLF 255.

[64] Frédéric Mégret and Marika Giles Samson, 'Holding the Line on Complementarity in Libya: The Case for Tolerating Flawed Domestic Trials' (2013) 11 JICJ 571.

[65] ibid 571.

[66] ibid 571, 577.

jurisdictions.[67] Greater support for domestic prosecutions would still deliver justice for victims and the protection of individuals. At the same time, it could remove the postcolonial frame created by a trial at The Hague.

This approach to complementarity could be argued to have very little to do with the authority of the ICC, but there are two responses to such criticism. Firstly, this would further secure the rule of law in respect of international criminal law. The ICC is the method by which justice is dispensed, but it does not create the law nor is it required for every exercise of power in relation to international criminal law. It is the main vehicle for the enforcement of the law, and the key principles have now been codified by the Rome Statute, but the ICC is not and should not be viewed as the ultimate arbiter of international criminal law.

Secondly, the way in which African States have chosen to self-refer to the Court is possibly beyond the expectations of the drafters of the Statute.[68] This is largely because of the transitional situation many States find themselves in, confronted with a variety of issues from funding their judicial systems to instability generated by armed conflict. Domestic prosecutions, in such situations, have been argued by the States concerned to be all but impossible. However, some domestic prosecutions in certain cases have been achievable. In the case of Mbarushimana, the reasoning by the Democratic Republic of the Congo to refer while undertaking domestic prosecutions was not really clear,[69] other than to say that they intended to exercise jurisdiction over a certain number of crimes before the date of referral.[70] It may have been the case that private negotiations concluded that this was the best way forward, but a clear basis on which to share jurisdiction would have added to the Court's authority here. Consequently, a more formal sharing of jurisdiction in such cases, or a hybridised approach which prioritises trial at the domestic level with ICC support, would perhaps better support the aims of complementarity. This would then allow the ICC to focus on maintaining a good relationship with all States, including non-States Parties,[71] to support the development of national prosecution mechanisms and cooperation more broadly between States.

67 Austin and Thieme (n 33) 342, 348.

68 Mégret and Samson (n 64) 571.

69 Defence challenge to the jurisdiction of the Court, *The Prosecutor v Callixte Mbarushimana* ICC-01/04-01/10 19 July 2011.

70 ibid, paras 16–20.

71 Ovo Imoedemhe, 'Unpacking the Tension between the African Union and the International Criminal Court: The Way Forward' (2015) 23 AJICL 74.

There is an interesting suggestion that the UN General Assembly should take responsibility for referrals[72] to the ICC, rather than the UNSC. While this may make the referral more democratic, or less influenced by power politics, it is simply not the role of the General Assembly to take such an active, engaged interest in matters of peace and security. Chapter IV of the UN Charter provides several express limitations on the ability of the General Assembly to act in relation to matters of peace and security and requires that it typically defer in such cases to the Security Council. Because of the nature of their separate remits, the General Assembly is not able to simply take over certain roles from the UNSC. The permanent five members of the UNSC thus continue to wield significant power over the referral system to the ICC, which is problematic given that three of the members have prolific colonial histories. This is thus one aspect of the postcolonial dimension to international criminal law which remains, and which has the power to undermine the authority of international criminal law.

The use of a stronger version of positive complementarity supports the development of justice through the Court, strengthening its authority without undermining the domestic judicial systems and creating, in the words of Amann, a post-postcolonial world of no accountability.[73] In her view, the role of African, and other postcolonial, States, is growing in a way to demonstrate that 'we are all postcolonials now'[74] and thus that the new world order needs to ensure that accountability is placed at the centre of its aims. However, this disregards the problems associated with recent attempts at complementarity. The situation in Kenyatta and in Kenya more generally was a poor indication of how complementarity might work; it was considered by many scholars to have undermined the authority of the ICC significantly because of the way in which the situation was handled. From this perspective, however, the Court and the law in general was not undermined because of the behaviour of Kenyatta or the refusal of the ICC to allow the cases to be tried in Kenya. The failure remains the inability to provide justice for victims; a failure which goes beyond the ICC and challenges the authority of international criminal law more generally.

The African Union has moved in a coordinated way towards a form of complementarity with the adoption of international criminal jurisdiction at the African Court for Justice and Human Rights.[75] The protocol amends the

[72] Cowell (n 43) 667, 687.

[73] Diane Marie Amann, 'The Post-Postcolonial Woman or Child' (2015) 30 AUIL 41.

[74] ibid 41, 43.

[75] Protocol on the Statute of the African Court of Justice and Human Rights 1 July 2008.

Statute of the Court by including a number of international crimes, including genocide[76] and aggression[77] within its jurisdiction, as well as a number of others not included in the Rome Statute, such as unconstitutional change of government[78] and drug trafficking.[79] There are concerns that there will be an overlap of jurisdiction[80] and the more significant criticism that 'duplicating' international systems should not be prioritised at the expense of the development of national criminal prosecutions.[81] This again accords with the idea that the ICC, potentially in conjunction with the African Court, should focus on domestic prosecutions and capacity-building mechanisms. This is supported by the arguments of TWAIL scholars, including those of Jalloh, Reynolds, and Xavier cited earlier, which consider the importance of developing domestic mechanisms and supporting prosecution at the local level as best as possible. The duplication of systems could be avoided by open lines of communication between the two, and a supportive approach from the ICC to the use of domestic prosecutions as a suitable alternative to international prosecution.

It is worth concluding this point by noting that the scientific origin of complementarity[82] aimed towards completeness, to explain why there were gaps emerging when a problem was examined from different perspectives. The idea that both perspectives remedied the deficiencies of the other to allow for a complete understanding of the problem is worth considering; the idea of complementarity is to ensure that prosecution does take place. At present, the deficiencies of international prosecution, and the difficulties it has had with authority, could be remedied by a greater focus on domestic prosecutions. The aim of completeness accords well with the aim of ending impunity, without the reliance on the ICC which has been demonstrated by some African States thus far. Whether this takes a hybridised approach, greater connections with local prosecutorial teams, or a bolder strategy which supports capacity-building in developing countries remains to be seen. The focus, however, should remain on a complete approach to justice which assures the victims that their voices will be heard, and that their experience matters. The judgment from Ongwen identified the importance of the victims to the Court

76 Article 28A(1), Statute of the African Court for Justice and Human Rights.

77 Article 28A(14), Statute of the African Court for Justice and Human Rights.

78 Article 28A(4), Statute of the African Court for Justice and Human Rights.

79 Article 28A(11), Statute of the African Court for Justice and Human Rights.

80 Zekarias Beshah Abebe, 'The African Court with a Criminal Jurisdiction and the ICC: A Case for Overlapping Jurisdiction' (2017) 25 AJICL 418.

81 Ademola Abass, 'The Proposed International Criminal Jurisdiction for the African Court: Some Problematical Aspects' (2013) 60 NILR 27.

82 Arkady Plotnitsky, *Nils Bohr and Complementarity: An Introduction* (Springer 2012).

by recounting, in incredible detail, the witness testimony to the Court.[83] International criminal law must continue to focus on the victims to ensure its own authority and continuation, for the protection of future victims.

6.5 CONCLUSION

From a Western or Euro centric perspective, the Court, and international criminal law more generally, has been identified as a public good, an aim which should be underpinned by all States. Both support the international rule of law and aim to support the maintenance of peace and security internationally. The support for the Court financially is derived mainly from richer, more powerful States and those who are generally subject to prosecutions have mainly originated from African States. This leads to repeated allegations that the Court is anti-African and that it displays such egregious bias that it undermines its own authority and credibility. It is entirely accurate that it is funded largely by Western powers. It is also fundamentally accurate that it has mainly prosecuted nationals of African States. However, the truth of whether it is biased against African States remains, as ever, more complex than such reductive conclusions would indicate. As discussed earlier, the problem of postcolonialism is significant; if we are all postcolonials, as Amann notes, then why has every State which has been accused of committing war crimes not been subject to the scrutiny of the Court? The roots of statehood, of the use of sovereignty as a shield for the 'civilising' powers which were guilty of the most brutal oppression history has seen, indicate that the roots of the problem go beyond a simple east and west dichotomy. The wealthy and settled nature of Western States relied on the exploitation of colonised peoples and the making of an international system in their image. To disregard this as a genuine concern for non-Western States before the Court is to fail to understand the power in the arguments of anti-African bias.

The number of prosecutions of African men before the Court lends credence to this complaint; it has been, thus far, a Court which tries Africans. However, the number of self-referrals by African States suggests that their perception of the Court's bias is not that strong. Domestic governments, such as the Democratic Republic of the Congo, have opted to send certain cases to the Court and to prosecute others domestically. There appears to be little significant concern at the domestic level that Africans are unduly targeted by the Court; a position supported by Bensouda, as the outgoing Prosecutor, that the Court supports

[83] *Prosecutor v Dominic Ongwen* ICC-02/04-01/15, 4 February 2021, *see*, for one example among many, paras 1326–1369.

African victims and prioritises them where otherwise there would be no justice. However, the problem is not so easily resolved, as was demonstrated by the discussion of the Kenyatta case. Consequently, greater reference should be made to the use of TWAIL scholarship, which underscores the importance of domestic prosecutions and domestic systems more generally. The removal of justice from the domestic environment may undermine the idea that justice is seen to be done by the victims and, consequently, and undermine the concept of justice overall. Moreover, the role of complementarity was not intended to allow domestic entities to choose when to prosecute, but rather to support justice for victims. A selective approach to complementarity, as discussed earlier and in previous chapters, is damaging to the aspirations the Court has in respect of justice and its task of ending impunity.

If such an approach to complementarity is necessary, it may be worth investigating the ways in which a fuller, more active version of complementarity could be pursued. The idea of complementarity as completeness could be undertaken by the Court, focusing on the delivery of justice by several means. This would involve not restricting the aims of the court to international or regional prosecution. The court's ability to support domestic prosecutions could go beyond a watching brief and focus on the ways in which capacity-building exercises could be undertaken by the Court to ensure the delivery of justice for local victims. The movement by the African Court to acquire jurisdiction is laudable in aiming towards this completeness, but it does not address the problem of the Court's authority more generally or the problem of removing justice from the local context. There will also remain the problems of ensuring domestic prosecutions which increase capacity, allowing domestic governments to build authority, and holding to account those who have committed serious crimes against local populations. Less focus on positive complementarity and more on an active form of complementarity would support this aim to develop a complete system of justice, where the norm is domestic prosecution. This would also go some way to repairing the scars of colonialism and to truly supporting the development of developing countries. This should then avoid their characterisation in the continuous present forever, which has undermined their ability to protect local populations. This approach could form the basis for a theory of authority of international criminal law.

7

A Theory of Authority of International Criminal Law

7.1 INTRODUCTION

The discussion in Chapter 6 demonstrated that the controversy of authority is less contentious at the international level, because of the presumed power of international institutions and the States which have created them. However, once the roots of that power are explored, contentious issues emerge. The link between authority and legitimacy supports an understanding of authority as intrinsically connected to the idea of legitimacy; authority flows only from exercises of power which are legitimate, requiring the reason for the exercise of that power to be explored and justified. At the domestic level, there is a reasonably straightforward solution for this, in that the legitimacy of the government can be explored through the way in which it is constituted, the way in which it adheres to the Constitution or constitutional norms, and the way in which it exercises its power. The problem becomes more complex in general international law because there is a lack of central authority, but also because of the nature of specific areas, such as international criminal law, which place limits on the ability of sovereign States to act. These limitations are necessary in a system which seeks to undermine impunity, to support justice for victims, but there does not seem to be a clear way of understanding when and whether certain acts can be considered legitimate. The authority of such acts in a general international law sense is problematic: theories of context-dependent authority, of variable, contested authority, and those which apply with relative ease to the national level, fall short in the context of international criminal law. There are limited explanations for ideas such as referrals by the UNSC and exercises of complementarity, which appear convoluted and inconsistent in their exercise.

The solution is not to submit to incoherence, but to look at where the exercises of power demonstrate consistency, as well as the overall aims of the system. Ultimately, the authority of international criminal law cannot be rooted too deeply in sovereignty or State consent, because of the issues this creates in the postcolonial context in which the international system operates. Despite the views of some, we remain, as a world, postcolonial, and a failure to acknowledge this may not undermine financial or trade systems but is likely to have a far greater impact on areas of public international law. Specifically, it has a detrimental impact on international criminal justice. International criminal justice relies on domestic support, through exercise or belief, to achieve its aims. Justice cannot be seen to be done where the domestic population believe that the power is being exercised in a neo-colonial fashion.

The purpose of this chapter is to set out the findings of the project and the theory of authority. Originally, the hypothesis of this project was founded on the idea that international criminal law's authority was circular, leading back to State consent. A later investigation posited that it could be founded on the existence of a system of principles. Although this could be the case, the conclusions reached based on this research indicate that the authority of international criminal law is based exclusively on the concept of justice, the ability to deliver justice, and the protection of the rights of victims. This theory acknowledges the Eurocentric roots of the discipline, while appreciating that international criminal justice is a branch of public international law. It also takes in an understanding of the postcolonial world, the focus of the Court on Africa, and the way in which law should be rooted in service to populations, rather than in service to lawmakers. This approach to authority also allows for course correction when the ICC seeks to undermine its own authority by taking an imbalanced approach to situations in different parts of the world.

This chapter looks firstly at the problem of authority linked to both State consent and the Charter. Drawing on the previous discussion of postcolonialism, the State and the ability of the UNSC to make referrals to the Court, the argument will be put forward that these remain an unstable, and potentially destabilising, foundation on which to base authority. The lack of a clear basis requires a different theoretical approach. The next part to the discussion looks at the idea of authority rooted in both justice and rights, discussing the development of international criminal justice alongside the human rights movement, and the way in which the justification for following such rules is rooted in an understanding of the rules serving the international population, particularly those vulnerable to atrocity crimes and victims of previous crimes. The last part to the chapter looks at the implications for a theory of authority based on rights for areas such as positive complementarity and UNSC referrals, and how these areas may need to adjust to conform to an understanding of authority which supports the legitimate exercise of power in this area. As is frequently noted, should the Court's main aim be to end impunity, it should move towards a complete approach to complementarity. This completeness should involve the generalised support for domestic prosecutions to ensure that its exercises of power are truly legitimate, and that its aims are fulfilled at both the international and the national level.

7.2 THE PROBLEM WITH AUTHORITY BASED ON STATE CONSENT AND THE UN CHARTER

The earlier discussions, in Chapters 5 and 6, around postcolonialism, provided a critical perspective on the utility of deferring to the authority of States and the UN Charter when discerning the authority of international criminal law. In particular, the question of UNSC referrals, under the Rome Statute, could be said to undermine the authority of the Court by deferring to the permanent five members, at least three of whom have colonised significant parts of the world. Drawing on the previous discussion of postcolonialism, the State and the UN Charter as the source of authority on which UNSC referrals can be made to the Court, the argument will be put forward that these remain an unstable, and potentially destabilising, foundation on which to base authority. The lack of a clear basis requires a different theoretical approach, focusing instead on the way in which State consent and the UN Charter should not be considered the basis of authority for international criminal law.

In the view of van Roermund, there is no order outwith the sovereign order of States[1] and the law at any given time is shaped by the present lawmakers, who identify principles and agree to them.[2] While Kant posited the idea that membership of the international community should be predicated on liberal values and democracy,[3] modern States do not wish to step outside the international community because they view the liberal and democratic values as being key to their civilised nature, even where this remains something of a façade. As Kolb notes, these rules are of direct benefit to the State, otherwise they would not obey the norms.[4] The benefit identified here is the continued membership of the community and the respect due to a powerful State without it having to demand that respect by force. In this way, some forms of public international law have greater power over States than others, and

1 Bert van Roermund, 'Instituting Authority: Some Kelsenian Notes' (2002) 15 RJ 206, 216.

2 Robert Kolb, 'Discussion of TH Cheng's Monograph When International Law Work, and in Particular a Defence of the Nicaragua Judgment of the ICJ' (2013) 26 LJIL 751, 752.

3 Immanuel Kant, *Perpetual Peace* (first published 1795, Hackett 2003).

4 Kolb (n 2) 751, 752.

international criminal law is one such. As Raymond notes, the normative expectations which are created by international law give an indication of how States ought to behave, and violations of these expectations can be regarded as a guide of how the State in question may behave in the future.[5] This can also be identified as a duty of obedience to international law on the part of States, with the underlying moral obligation to which that alludes.[6] Kumm goes on to highlight that respect for norms such as those of international criminal law demonstrates a continuation for the respect already in existence for the domestic constitutional values in liberal democracies.[7] As such, the international values reflect and support the domestic values adhered to by these States. Although the State may have the ultimate power to act as it wishes, arbitrary power is limited by its authority to act. Those parameters are, as constitutional law is, a self-imposed limit on the State's power to act. The State adheres to this limitation out of a desire for membership of the community and to maintain it's external reputation. Although this demonstrates more clearly that international law is thus a form of ethics created by States to establish a common standard of behaviour, it is their treatment of these rules that gives them the legal quality they possess. For international criminal law in particular, this legal quality, or the legal element thereto, means that the norms regarding the criminalisation of certain acts and the rules concerning the treatment of non combatants have endured despite numerous breaches over time. Thus, the authority of international law is a self-imposed recognition of the legitimate limits within which power may be exercised, and a desire to maintain these limits, broadly.

The limits are characterised by support and membership of the UN Charter, which would make the source of authority of international criminal law, and indeed all public international law, the UN Charter. States have consented to these norms, but the source of authority is neither consent or the UN Charter, as discussed in Chapters 3 and 4. Fassbender's notion of constitutionalism, in that it is set out by the UN Charter,[8] is flawed without a recognition of the role of power and the way in which certain States are privileged over others. Arguably, the combination of the UN Charter and State consent as the root of the authority of international criminal law is an

5 Gregory A Raymond, 'Problems and Prospects in the Study of International Norms' (1997) 41 MISR 205, 217.

6 Mattias Kumm, 'The Legitimacy of International Law: A Constitutionalist Framework of Analysis' (2004) 15 EJIL 907, 908.

7 ibid 907, 917.

8 Johannes Gerald Van Mulligen, 'Global Constitutionalism and the Objective Purport of the International Legal Order' (2011) 24 LJIL 277, 286.

unstable basis on which to base the authority of the law precisely because of the fluctuations in power (albeit among the same grouping of States) which have played a role in the development of the law, and the way in which it continues to affect the law at an international level. As Kolb wisely highlights, the 'law as a living thing . . . is shaped by the decision-maker exclusively in the particular situation'[9] and States, admittedly certain States, have been at the centre of the development of international criminal law. The idea that States are bound to uphold certain values may be true and enforceable at the domestic level,[10] but bears little relationship to the situation at the international level. Moreover, the postcolonial context is ignored by such arguments; it presumes the world to be shaped in a, most likely, European, way.

Taking together the concept of authority as a legitimate exercise of power and the difficulty of proving that at the international level, as discussed in Chapters 2 and 3, it becomes apparent that other bases for authority, such as global constitutionalism via the UN Charter and the notion of State consent as the justification for the exercise of power, fall short, particularly in the context of international criminal justice. The concept of international criminal law as ideology[11] further undermines its authority. As discussed previously, there is a lack of balance when international criminal law is applied. The postcolonial context, and the destabilising effect of colonialism, means that there is more likely to be instability in certain parts of the world, such as Africa, and that international criminal law has consequently been focused more on this geographical area. However, the question is not one of focusing on the wrong continent, but a failure to focus on the abuse of power which characterises serious violations of international criminal law. The alleged war crimes in both Iraq and Afghanistan concern Western States which have not accounted for the damage caused, either in court or by way of formal recognition and apology. The point that a country's decision to follow international law reflects a assessment that the costs of a violation outweigh the benefits[12] is rendered moot in international criminal law; the operation of sovereignty and complementarity undermines compliance through an obfuscating engagement with complementarity, as seen in the case of the British government. The focus by Western governments on improving institutions is laudable, but it does not

[9] Kolb (n 2) 751, 752.

[10] Thomas Kleinlein, 'On Holism, Pluralism, and Democracy: Approaches to Constitutionalism beyond the State' (2010) 21 EJIL 1075, 1077–1078.

[11] Shirley V Scott, 'International Law as Ideology: Theorizing the Relationship between International Law and International Politics' (1994) 5 EJIL 313.

[12] Andrew Guzman, 'A Compliance-Based Theory of International Law' (2002) 90 Cal L Rev 1823, 1853

support the overall aims of international criminal justice. Instead, it gives the well-evidenced perspective that certain States can use sovereignty as something of a shield, and consequently, that the global constitutional order is worth little when it confronts wealth and power.

In the context of developing a theory of authority that makes sense of what international criminal justice does, and which connects well with its aspirations to end impunity and protect vulnerable individuals from the worst atrocities, it is necessary to take account of the postcolonial context. The shape of international law and the UN Charter was cast by those States which undertook brutal 'civilising' missions, for the purpose of extracting resources, across the world. It is no wonder that there is a degree of suspicion around the new language of ending impunity. The UN Charter, and State consent more broadly, is therefore unsuitable as a basis for the authority of international criminal law.

However, considering the purpose of international criminal justice, and a more complete approach to complementarity that views the role of the Court as supportive rather than interventionist, the basis of the Court's authority can be viewed differently. Rather than a focus on its role as an international institution funded and supported by Western States who are reluctant to support investigations of their own forces, its role as an institution founded for the protection of individuals and the rights of victims, and the delivery of justice to victims, is a more constructive basis. Such a basis allows for a fuller understanding of the Court's role in the international system and provides an answer to the problem of autonomy in the context of criminal law. The focus on the provision of justice, rather than the consent of States, would also explain the role of the UNSC in referring cases, while setting out limits for its ability to do so, considering the way in which it may act without power where justice is not served. Placing the victims at the heart of the international system is something that the Court is beginning to do in practice,[13] a direction which supports its overall mission. The next part to the discussion looks at the idea of authority rooted in both justice and rights, discussing the development of international criminal justice alongside the human rights movement, and the way in which the justification for following such rules in rooted in an understanding of the rules serving the international population, particularly those vulnerable to atrocity crimes and victims of previous crimes.

[13] *Prosecutor v Dominic Ongwen* ICC-02/04-01/15, 4 February 2021, see, for one example among many, paras 1326–1369.

7.3 AUTHORITY AS JUSTICE

The idea of justice and rights being connected is developed by the work of David Luban, in his discussion of the 'tandem' development of international criminal law and human rights. He notes that the focus in the beginning was on collectives and moved gradually to individual rights,[14] although arguably this was a key part of the concepts driving international criminal law, which focused on the individual responsibility of those who had contributed to the commission of atrocities during the Second World War. This connection offered legitimacy to both international criminal law and international human rights law; both were rooted in the protection of individuals, and so could be justified where the protection was required. The right to create such rights was ascribed to States at the international level, derived from their power to make law more generally. This connects to Buchanan's understanding of normative legitimacy[15] as a right to rule, rather than the sociological form which connotes acceptance by those over whom the authority is exercised.

This demonstrates a Razian understanding of authority: that the party with authority has the right to take and to make decisions because others have reasons to follow them. The constitutional basis has less of an impact than the knowledge that the members of the State, specifically the population, will follow it. However, Raz's ideas indicate an overwhelming, overriding moralism in the choices made by the population. The power that the State has over the individuals is cemented by the ability to change the laws, and the adherence of the State to the rule of law is conditional only on the State actors' conscience.

More recent scholarship develops this approach by focusing on the State's responsibility as, variously, 'trustees of humanity'[16] and 'fiduciaries of humanity.'[17] In the latter work, characterising States as the guardians of such ideas, Fox-Decent and Criddle focus on the roots of their work in that of both Vattel and Lauterpacht, placing responsibility for the guardianship of areas as varied as the use of natural resources to prosecution for atrocity crimes squarely on the

[14] David Luban, 'Fairness to Rights: Jurisdiction, Legality and the Legitimacy of International Criminal Law' in John Tasioulas and Samantha Besson (eds), *The Philosophy of International Law* (Oxford University Press 2010), 574.

[15] Allen Buchanan, 'The Legitimacy of International Law' in John Tasioulas and Samantha Besson (eds), *The Philosophy of International Law* (Oxford University Press 2010).

[16] Eyal Benvenisti, 'Sovereigns as Trustees of Humanity: On the Accountability of States to Foreign Stakeholders' (2013) 107 AJIL 295.

[17] Evan Criddle and Evan Fox-Decent, *Fiduciaries of Humanity: How International Law Constitutes Authority* (Oxford University Press 2016).

shoulders of States. Returning to Kolb's idea of a direct benefit,[18] which is absent where certain areas contribute to a better world, rather than directly impacting on immediate State interests, these ideas can be viewed in part as utopian, perhaps rooted in a classical 'is-ought' approach, and characterising States as how they ought to be, rather than how they are.

As discussed earlier, the obligations States have in respect of rights and justice are not necessarily upheld to the same degree; there is little an international court can do beyond adjudicating the case and, in the case of the European Court of Human Rights, imposing a fine. The earlier chapters discussed both the value of sovereignty across different nations and examined the idea of sovereignty as a postcolonial concept. Taken together, reliance on statehood to uphold rights and protect justice would be naïve at best, and at worst, has undermined the system. This can be seen clearly in the movement by the African Union to withdraw from the ICC, viewing it as too biased against their members and too focused on a Eurocentric approach to international criminal law, despite the self-referrals which have been made by African States for prosecutions by the ICC. It is possible to view sovereignty as contingent on respect for rights, but again this is not evidenced broadly at the international level.[19] Consequently, the focus should remain on the institution's authority as distinct from that of individual States and members, and how it can be seen as authoritative when exercising power, via jurisdiction or through other means. The authority of international criminal law, and the ICC, should be based on the protection of individuals vulnerable to atrocity crimes and the delivery of justice for such victims. This dynamic approach to authority appreciates the developing nature of international law, which may change depending on the actors in charge at that time.[20] It also founds the legitimacy of the exercises of power by the international criminal law on the individual, rather than relating it to States. As demonstrated earlier, sovereignty as a concept evidently is not supportive of international criminal justice and its role in the colonial context has undermined faith and respect for international law. It also creates an impunity gap for those who would seek to exploit it, by relating arguments of neo-colonialism to greater respect for Western States than for African States.

[18] Kolb (n 2) 751, 752.

[19] Buchanan (n 15) 79–96, 95.

[20] Peter J Katzenstein, 'States and Power as Ur-Force: Domestic Traditions and Embedded Actors in World Politics' 139–156, 147 in Martha Finnemore and Judith Goldstein (eds), *Back to Basics: State Power in a Contemporary World* (Oxford University Press 2013), 147.

This approach is typified by the Kenyatta case, in which the postcolonial weaknesses of the Court were suitably exploited by a powerful individual and successfully undermined the prosecution. The victims of violence have not yet seen justice; such a focus roundly undermines the idea that the Court is neo-colonial in its intentions or that it is a tool for Western States. Authority as justice asks the question of when the victims will receive justice and how that will happen, be it at the international or domestic level. A clear, purposive focus places the burden on the shoulders of those who seek to shield themselves from the Court, and the exercise of the law more broadly, to answer as to how victims will be supported. Sovereignty becomes less important than discharging the responsibilities thereof; a point the work previously referenced attempts to make, without adequately considering the postcolonial context.

This view of authority would appear potentially utopian were it not for such a context. The damage colonial powers have done to the world is not irreparable, but the debt remains unsettled. A view beyond the significance of sovereignty, the interests of individual States, and their identities[21] supports the move towards Amann's post-postcolonial society, the roots of which are only beginning to take hold. A focus on justice and the protection of individuals as the basis for authority would also query the use of complementarity by the Court and explore its potential for support.

The question of complementarity, as discussed earlier, is both supportive of the basis of authority as justice and could also undermine it, if a balanced, constructive approach to complementarity is not undertaken. The view that complementary prosecutions at the ICC can be used by States who wish to selectively prosecute, without adequate justification for doing so, goes beyond the intention of the drafters. Moreover, it utilises the Court in a way which is open to criticism; it prioritises certain victims in an arbitrary fashion, without explaining why certain situations should be examined, investigated, or whether certain cases should be built. The argument here is not for greater explanation of prosecutorial discretion, but rather a more balanced approach. The idea that the UK government, in prosecuting precisely one individual accused of war crimes in Iraq, has discharged its obligations in respect of justice for the victims is deeply questionable. Moreover, two investigations of the one situation should have yielded more than concluding the investigation without further monitoring. The approach here contrasts sharply with the other situations which were previously under examination and have been concluded; there remains a basis, but the UK government have simply

[21] Harold Hongju Koh, 'Why Do Nations Obey International Law?' (1997) 106 Yale LJ 2599, 2652.

obfuscated more effectively than their postcolonial counterparts. Even maintaining a watching brief on the situation, to apply a certain degree of pressure, would have been more balanced than simply admitting defeat because of the failure to secure evidence at such an early stage in the proceedings. As noted earlier, it is inexplicable that the ICC should monitor some States and ignore others. The authority of the ICC requires a measured, balanced approach, particularly towards powerful States, which is underpinned by its motivation to secure justice. This is the root of its authority; the focus on justice for victims in every situation, not just those which provide a relatively, and it is indeed a case of being relatively, smoother path to trial.

As discussed, this idea of authority as justice could then be used to analyse the way in which the ICC, as the primary vehicle for international criminal law, can support the fuller use of complementarity at the domestic level. The next part to this discussion focuses on the way in which positive complementarity can be used to underpin justice as authority, and underscores the earlier discussion of a fuller, more complete approach to complementarity. The role of UNSC referrals is also relevant, in that such a theory could both challenge and support the use of referrals in the context of atrocity crimes.

7.4 IMPLICATIONS OF AUTHORITY AS JUSTICE

Justifications for the concept of authority as rooted in justice have a number of dimensions in practice: not only does this transfer the roots of authority from sovereignty and sovereign States to the purpose of the institution and the exercise of its power, moving towards a 'complete' understanding of complementarity, it also has implications for UNSC referrals under the Statute, and how these may or may not conform to an understanding of authority which supports the legitimate exercise of power in the area. If the Court's main aim is to eradicate impunity, its aim should be towards a more complete approach to complementarity, engaging with more and generalised support for domestic prosecutions to ensure that it exercises power in a truly legitimate way. This would also fulfil its aims at the international and national level, supporting a more active approach to ending impunity.

As Franck notes, legitimacy must be earned over time. The perception of legitimacy possessed by sovereign States, particularly those with great power, is not necessarily relevant in the context of international criminal justice. In respect of universalism and civilisation, its pedigree is questionable. A movement towards the institution as a separate entity which focuses on its purpose, rather than the direction of or evasion by individual States, would support the idea of exercising power in a legitimate fashion. It could then focus on building up a bank of legitimacy, through acts which demonstrate an even-handed and truly universal approach. This could be carried out by focusing more clearly on the victims who have suffered and the likelihood that they will achieve justice in their own States. Where the victims are likely to be left without access to justice, the Court could then step in to provide a path to prosecution. At present, the moment at which they step in generally reflects the passing of authority and responsibility to the Court, rather than engagement with the domestic authorities. Although there may be greater engagement behind the scenes, when responsibility is transferred, there is little further development at the domestic level. Moreover, it is not clear as to why certain States would use complementarity, in the sense of transferring the prosecution to the international level, as a means of filling highly specific gaps. This again prioritises certain victims over others, without focusing on the gravity of the crimes. A more active approach to complementarity may be required, to accord with the notion of authority. Rather than relying on the removal of the obligation to prosecution, supported domestic prosecutions, capacity-building endeavours, and a recognition that the domestic trial is desirable for the provision of local, visible justice may be the necessary direction of complementarity for the Court. This allows for a clear, focused approach to the provision of justice, honouring the nature of complementarity as a means of ensuring prosecution, rather than taking over the obligations of domestic States.

The African Court's attempts to secure jurisdiction for international prosecutions is interesting, but still transfers the obligation from the national to the regional level. This is not active complementarity in the way viewed by this work, in that prosecution at the domestic level should be supported. A move away from international prosecutions and towards greater engagement with the domestic government encourages a focus on authority as justice, holding that the main aim of the Court is not to enshrine the existing order in law, but to truly end impunity.

The other implication for the concept of justice as authority to be discussed here is the role of UNSC referrals. Although only two referrals have been made thus far, with the armed conflict in Libya and the alleged genocide and crimes against humanity in Darfur being referred to the Court, it is still an exercise of power by the UNSC which affects the authority of the Court. There is no clearer example of that than the attempted referral of Syria in 2014, which was blocked by two members of the permanent five of the UNSC.[22]

[22] The situation in Darfur, UNSC Resolution S/RES/1593 of 31 March 2005, 1 and the situation in Libya, UNSC Resolution S/RES/1970 of 26 February 2011.

The failure of the State to protect civilians in Syria; the generalised failure to adequately maintain its borders, particularly in relation to Northern Iraq; and the lack of capacity in both countries to try individuals who are accused of some of the most serious violations of international criminal law are unquestionably a failure to secure justice for these victims. Yet the inability of the UNSC to refer the case on geopolitical grounds undermines the function of the referral mechanism. It feeds into the debate about the selective nature of examinations and investigations at the Court, supporting the notion that the interests of great powers are more important than individual victims. Through the lens of authority as justice, such referrals fail to support the authority of the Court and demonstrate themselves as exercises of power by powerful entities. In this case, the denial of a referral supports the lack of authority of the process; referrals may be made and denied at the will of powerful actors, having little regard for the mantle of peace and security under which they act.

The greatest support for the legitimacy of the acts of the ICC, as the main vehicle for international criminal law, thus rests with the Court itself and its engagement with domestic governments. A reduced focus on international prosecution and more support for domestic action would develop the Court's authority, as acting legitimately and in the interests of justice for victims. The referral mechanism for the UNSC may act as a safety net in the view of some scholars but fails to support the authority of the Court. Instead, it creates the same problems as a reliance on statehood and sovereignty for authority in international criminal law. The role of power politics is too great; the focus on victims and justice is insufficient. A more balanced approach to referrals would need to be mandated, which is not possible within the current system. Neither is it necessarily desirable; a significant change to the way in which the UNSC works would have other implications which should be carefully considered, and which are beyond the scope of this work. With a more active approach to complementarity, in respect of both non-States Parties and States Parties, complementarity could replace referrals, which are barely used at present, in any case. Authority as justice is not perfect, but it does explain the role of the Court beyond the excessive language in the Preamble and the way in which the Court can ensure that its focus remains on those who are affected most greatly by serious violations of international criminal law.

7.5 CONCLUSION

In an unstable, postcolonial world, the ICC has an extensive workload which appears to be growing with each decade. Its ability to act legitimately, not only in a lawful, textual sense of complying with the Statute, is critical for the fulfilment of its mission. The discussion in previous chapters focused on the difficulty of asserting authority in the context of freedom, where autonomy is prized, in the context of a system predicated on will, such as international law, and in a postcolonial word, where noble concepts such as civilisation were used to brutalise and exploit populations. This makes the task of describing and delineating authority difficult, but not impossible: the use of power by the ICC, and international criminal law more generally, must be in the service of justice for victims. Any deviation from that path will lack legitimacy and would therefore not be a legitimate exercise of power. Characterising authority as justice is not even as remotely utopian as it may seem. Instead, it adds a necessary practical dimension to the Court's work and has implications for several aspects of its work.

Firstly, it offers a description of authority which does not require roots in either State consent or the UN Charter. This is critical because of the post-colonial context, as well as the more generalised problem of State consent at the international level. Secondly, authority as justice focuses on the purpose of the ICC, and international criminal law more broadly. Lastly, it honours the history of the discipline, as requiring accountability to the victims of atrocities by the perpetrators. The way in which this is satisfied is through engagement with two key areas: UNSC referrals and the doctrine of complementarity.

The reliance on State consent and the UN Charter for authority is detrimental to the authority of international criminal law because the States who fund the Court, and who were responsible for the creation of the first international criminal tribunals, were also responsible for significant damage through colonialism. Consequently, the idea of international criminal law can be easily, and basically, qualified as a neo-colonial project. Movement away from the reliance on State consent, and the UN Charter as a proxy therefore, would allow international criminal law to be justified without recourse to States. Instead, it has its own internal logic which supports justice for those who have been victimised by serious violations and avoids the characterisation, principally by those who do not wish to be prosecuted for well-evidenced abuses of power, of the Court as a neo-colonial endeavour. The conscious focus on authority as justice requires them to answer to the question of justice and leads to the second point regarding complementarity. By focusing on authority as justice, the Court should move beyond international prosecution to a greater focus on the domestic context and how it can support such prosecutions. A more even-handed approach to examinations and investigations, particularly watching briefs, undermines the focus of the Court as on Africa and instead focuses on the victims of atrocities, wherever and by whomever these may be committed. States with capacity for prosecution should be supported in their endeavours; international prosecution is not necessary in every single case.

The use of UNSCs referrals has been limited thus far; the restricted use of the mechanism demonstrates the political problems of guaranteeing a referral if all the permanent members are required to vote in favour of it. Equally, this demonstrates the limited authority that States, State consent, and the UN can have in such situations, if the issue must be submitted to the considerations of power politics. Such exercises are not in keeping with many definitions of authority and unquestionably lack the focus on justice that the authority of international criminal law should have. Accordingly, referrals may undermine the Court more than they support its aims; a more active approach to complementarity could, in time, replace the function of referrals and support the idea, truly, of the authority of criminal law as being rooted completely in justice for the victims.

8

Conclusion

8.1 AUTHORITY AND LEGITIMACY AT THE INTERNATIONAL LEVEL

The quiet controversy of authority as a concept has hopefully been demonstrated fully by now. Rather than an archaic jurisprudential concept, this work has aimed to demonstrate the significant implications that a failure to adequately understand and set out the authority of institutions in international criminal law could have. The question of legitimacy is redundant should there be no exploration of authority, and thus the initial discussion, which demonstrated the link between authority and legitimacy, provided a foundation for the discussion of, effectively, whether exercises of power in international criminal law can be viewed as legitimate. It remains curious that the concept of authority at the domestic level has been extensively debated, with a focus on the ability to determine the rules that others will follow. The initial idea, of authority as the ability to command, has been shown to be outdated and problematic for liberal democratic societies. Consideration of personal autonomy is required, to understand how power works in societies which protect freedom on a constitutional basis. Autonomy has been shown to be significant for the idea of authority at the domestic level and remains critical as an element of authority: commands can no longer be issued to the masses with the expectation of blind obedience. Engagement with individual freedom is key.

In a similar way, the element of legitimacy is critical: legitimate exercises of power confer authority and permit the acts which are being carried out to be considered as legitimate. However, the idea of legitimacy as a concept beyond mere lawfulness is important: it should instead be regarded as the basis for authority. Legitimate exercises of power which engage with individual autonomy will thus have authority. This cements the link between power, legitimacy, and authority: legitimacy is a condition of the exercise of power for it to be authoritative, and rules may not possess authority unless legitimacy underpins the exercise of such power. There must also be engagement with the autonomy of the free individuals within society. While this may work well, broadly, for areas such as contract law, there is a tension between this idea and the question of proscription under criminal law. The concept of autonomy is directly affected by criminal law, in which the ideas are not considered merely 'good advice,' but instead rules which can be met with harsh sanctions and significant social penalties, such as the permanent entry of one's name on an offender's register. The restrictions that criminal law places on individual autonomy are not only valid and necessary, particularly where the behaviour has a harmful impact on others, but must also be broadly accepted across societies. It is critical that criminal law possesses authority, accordingly.

As its legitimacy cannot be rooted in an engagement with personal autonomy, it must be justified in another way. The legitimacy of criminal law must rely on its balance of protection for the rights and freedoms of different members in society to achieve authority. As a method of justice, it aims to deter and prevent injury and misery, without which individuals would be able to act with impunity. To an extent, this works at the domestic level but there are greater challenges to authority for international criminal law. Consequently, the examination of authority in both public international law and international criminal law more specifically had to engage with conceptions of authority and the problems associated therewith.

The ability of States to create and issue rules at the international level is considered a key element of legal authority. The legitimacy of those acts is therefore linked to the domestic authority that States possess and the order which they represent: for public international law, the link between domestic orders and the international system is the basis for the authority of international law. The authority of State to create law and rules allows an understanding of the authority of the rules to be explained: their authority to make rules at the domestic level is transferred to the international level through the exercise of consent. This makes the exercise of their powers at that level legitimate. However, this would require consent for every legitimate exercise of power, and international law does not function in that way. Other aspects, such as morality, may confer authority on the acts of States. However, this point makes several assumptions, of which a clear understanding of morality and the equality of sovereign States are but two. The discussion in Chapter 3 used political theory to demonstrate the way in which sovereignty can offer privilege, as well as the extent to which it can identify powerful entities in certain circumstances. The power is thus vested in certain actors, who may be more influential than certain States. This does not result in authority, but their acts can have a significant impact on international law. This identifies a central problem with the State-based system. Morality ought to be able to provide a restraint for such exercises of power, but there does not appear to be a great deal of regard for morality in such circumstances, or any normative order external to that of the political system. Arguably, the recognition of human rights provides a check on exercises of power and could potentially indicate that authority is conferred on acts which respect the rights-based order of the international system. This is problematic, however, because even acts which lack legitimacy have an enduring influence and may change the international system because of the way in which such acts are considered State practice. The development in such cases may have a far-reaching effect on the legitimacy of acts, meaning that yesterday's act which lacked authority provides a basis on which to argue for the authority of tomorrow's act.

8.2 THE ROLE OF SOVEREIGNTY

Sovereignty and the rights-based order of the international system both have an enduring impact on the question of the authority of international law, but this does not necessarily address the specific issues created by international criminal law. International criminal law is a specific branch of public international law, and one which has several distinct considerations regarding authority, including the relatively recent creation of the ICC. The jurisdiction of the ICC is particularly problematic, because of the way in which referrals are made by the UNSC, as well as the possibility of self-referrals by both non-States Parties and States Parties. The key question is whether such exercises of power remain so or may be considered authoritative in the context of international criminal law.

The roots of international criminal law, in reference to the post-Second World War tribunals, did not make clear its source of authority, and there was no particular justification sought beyond the requirements of the UN structure to maintain peace and security. This highly general, and very new, concept was the basis for the creation of international criminal tribunals and has remained the basis for exercises of power in respect of the later ad hoc tribunals. Chapter 7 has been the justification for the creation of several both hybrid and international tribunals ever since. Similarly, the foundational argument for the Rome Statute, and its early development, was rooted in the UN's responsibility to maintain peace and security. However, the Rome Statute now stands alone as an international institution, with a specific connection to the idea of peace and security, although its authority is arguably primarily derived from the consent of State Parties. This remains the case until the Court's jurisdiction goes beyond those States which have consented to its jurisdiction, to States and situations involving other entities which have been referred to the Court by other States Parties and by the UNSC itself. This jurisdiction is much more expansive than that of previous international criminal tribunals, meaning that it goes beyond the UN powers to maintain peace and security and beyond the consent of States. This creates a difficulty in identifying exactly where the Court's authority may rest, as there is no clear designation of its authority. Instead, there are many general obligations in the preamble to the Statute, which set out the obligation to end impunity and to ensure that the interests of justice are met. Should the discussion of authority end now, the authority of such international criminal law would rest heavily on which tribunal was at issue and whether the individual before the Court possessed a jurisdictional link to a State Party. The role of power politics, accordingly, has a significant impact on the Court's exercises of power under the jurisdictional provisions of the Statute and is almost mandatory: the imperative to maintain peace and security via the UN, the understanding of the need for an international criminal court for the prosecution of serious violations of international criminal law, and the requirement that such a court be able to secure legitimacy through the delivery of justice and the protection of rights. However, these ideas cannot be realised without power and wealth, and the establishment of an order requires coordination and support. Few challenges have been made thus far to the jurisdiction or authority of the Court, and arguably no powerful nations have backed such challenges. No Western leaders or individuals from Western States have found themselves indicted by the Court thus far, despite investigations into the situations in Iraq and Afghanistan, both of which have extensively documented instances of the commission of war crimes. The role of sovereignty and complementarity in preventing prosecution is therefore critical to the discussion.

The authority of international criminal law cannot be vested solely in the consent of States and can be affected by power politics. Arguably, it rests in something more significant than the institution, potentially rooted in the focus on prosecuting the most serious crimes of concern to humanity. Identifying the central idea connected to this point, without dwelling on the slightly baroque language, this requires the ICC to focus on the most damaging cases and the situations which cause greatest concern to the international community, among other concerns. Article 17 allows the extension of that remit to situations in which a domestic prosecution is highly unlikely for reasons of unwillingness or inability, but the application of this rule has not been uniform. The case of the UK in Iraq sets a particularly concerning example because of the way in which the government has avoided and paid their way out of justice in Iraq, a country which is still struggling to re-establish itself following the invasion at the beginning of this century. Victims of war crimes have been compensated to varying degrees without any apology or admission of liability; the conduct of the British Army in making payments has been starkly at odds with their refusal to accept liability or even moral responsibility for the acts carried out by British soldiers while in Iraq.

The authority of international criminal law, accordingly, is not linked to States and their authority, per se, but rather the responsibility to hold those who carry out terrible crimes, particularly against civilians, to account. The accountability determines the existence of that authority: should the international justice system prove its fairness, justice must apply to all, without a privileged set of wealthy States putting forward assurances of their intention to investigate and prosecute publicly, while privately obstructing and preventing any slight risk of international humiliation. The demonstration by such States so far, using the example of the UK government, has been to prevent the indictment of any UK soldiers before the ICC. On the other hand, the Court does not seek to prosecute British soldiers if the domestic courts are able to take on the cases independently. The problem remains, however, that the British government have been unable to prosecute at the domestic level, meaning that the impunity gap which was noted in the Democratic Republic of Congo exists in the UK as well. The crimes committed by British soldiers, which were described during the trial of Donald Payne, indicate the way in which such individuals disregarded the life, the dignity, and the personhood of those under their charge. The inhuman treatment of prisoners, and in particular the open humiliation, was not carried out privately and discreetly by a few sadistic persons. Such treatment was open and widely acknowledged; the evidence corroborated the existence of witnesses to the conduct and the judge noted how difficult it was to appreciate, under such circumstances, that those in command would have no knowledge of such treatment of the prisoners. The existence of evidence to support the conclusion that those who were acting had done so without fear of reprisal or even mild chastisement, the approach of the UK government, and the concept of international criminal justice remain diametrically opposed. It is difficult to parse as to why this is not precisely the sort of situation in which the ICC ought to intervene.

The practicalities involved are not underestimated: acquiring evidence is always challenging, but more difficult cases have been launched, both politically and geographically, than in the case of the UK and Iraq. Numerous allegations were made and the Iraqi people could provide witness testimony. The potential to rely on such evidence, however, erodes slowly over time. As the years pass, the likelihood of prosecution may wither, along with the hope of justice for the victims of crimes. It is difficult to comprehend as to why certain

States ought to be monitored by the Court and why others are able to proceed as normal. The authority of the ICC requires balance in its approach, particularly in respect of powerful States. This balance does not yet exist: a far greater degree of trust is placed in wealthy, influential, and powerful States. Moreover, the approach undertaken in respect of the UK government provides a useful indication to future Western governments as to how they may avoid prosecution of their soldiers both at the international and domestic level. This is particularly concerning given the Australian government's role in Afghanistan and the current prosecutorial investigation into the situation there.

This approach would greatly undermine the Court's authority and support the argument that the Court is indeed a tool of postcolonial oppression. The anti-African bias which is frequently alleged by critics of the Court's approach would have greater substance where there has been a total lack of prosecution at both the international and national level for Western States, particularly where such States are Parties to the Rome Statute. This creates a significant issue for the Court's authority and undermines it from a postcolonial perspective.

The inherently 'good' nature, or at least intention, of international criminal law would be agreed by many Western, particularly European, nations, which have long supported the idea of an international criminal court. Broad Western support for the international criminal tribunals in the former Yugoslavia and Rwanda was evident through their creation by the UN Security Council, and the conception of an international criminal court received long-standing support from a variety of Western actors. The direct link between such tribunals and international peace and security generally has been acknowledged, and the greatest proof lies, as always, in the flow of financial might: financial support for the Court is derived mainly from richer, more powerful States. A simplistic view would regard this as deeply problematic, where those who fund are Western and those who are indicted are mainly African men. This is the basis for the argument that the Court is anti-African, that it is biased and therefore it cannot possess authority. However, despite its funding being drawn, largely, from richer States and although it is true that the prosecutions have mainly been of individuals from African States, the truth is more complex than it would initially appear. There are significant postcolonial issues, and we are not yet, as Amann has noted, all postcolonials. If we were, all States accused of war crimes would be subject to the equal and detailed scrutiny of the Court. The roots of statehood, in which the concept of sovereignty was used as a shield for the world powers who initially invaded and carved up so many countries around the world, for the purposes of, among other things, 'civilisation' and under the banner of which brutally oppressed indigenous populations, indicate that there is more to the problem than a simple dichotomy of North and South. The wealth and power of Western States was galvanised by the exploitation of those such States colonised, creating an international system which bore little relation to cultures outwith Europe. To ignore this significant concern in respect of nationals of African States who are indicted, based on a wealth of historical evidence, is to fail to understand the inherent strength of the argument of anti-African bias.

Most prosecutions thus far before the Court have been of African men, which lends credence to the complaint; it has been a Court for Africans to this point. However, to focus on those indicted is to ignore other considerations, such as the number of self-referrals which have been made by African States. This would indicate that the perception of the Court's bias is not as strong as one may think. Municipal governments, such as the Democratic Republic of the Congo, have sought a mixed approach: some cases go to the ICC, while others are prosecuted domestically. In this case, there is little evidence of a clear concern that African nationals and nations are unduly targeted by the Court. This point is made forcefully by Bensouda, former Prosecutor of the ICC, who noted that the Court was primarily supportive of African victims and prioritised them in situations where, without the Court, there would be no justice at all. Taking this together with TWAIL scholarship provides a more nuanced understanding of the problem, with the latter focusing on the importance of domestic prosecutions and attempts to strengthen domestic systems more generally. The withdrawal of justice from the domestic sphere can undermine the rule that justice must be seen to be done, particularly by victims, and could undermine the overall concept of justice. Furthermore, the idea of complementarity was not intended to offer governments the option to send certain cases to the ICC, and to pick and choose which to prosecute at home. This does not, and will not, support justice for victims. Selective complementarity, in this way, is broadly damaging to the aims of the Court and undermines its goals of ensuring justice for victims and ending impunity for international crimes.

8.3 AUTHORITY AS JUSTICE

Rather than leaving it entirely within the gift of States, the approach pursued by the Democratic Republic of the Congo may open possibilities for collaboration between domestic governments and the ICC. This could lead to a fuller, and possibly more active, version of complementarity, focusing on a complete approach to the doctrine by which justice could be delivered by several means. This would prevent the restriction of justice to international or regional prosecution and allow the Court to support domestic prosecutions more actively. This could go beyond a watching brief of governmental activity and focus on the ways in which the Court could support capacity-building to ensure that local victims are able to access justice and, critically, watch it in operation in a more familiar context. The movement by the African Court to acquire jurisdiction for international crimes is a constructive move towards completeness, but it does not address the problem of the Court's authority more generally. Equally, there is little consideration of the removal of justice from the local level, as a pan-continental regime will not be local to everyone. There remain the issues of ensuring that domestic prosecutions do indeed increase and support capacity, allowing domestic governments to build authority and generate a system of accountability for those who have committed serious crimes against local populations. A lesser focus on positive complementarity and a greater focus on a more active form of complementarity would support this aim, of developing a complete system of justice where the norm is domestic prosecution. Domestic prosecution should not be a privilege and such an approach may go a certain way to offer a degree of repair to the scars of colonialism, attempting to truly support the development of developing countries and avoiding their characterisation as such in the continuous present forever.

The instability of the world means that the ICC's extensive workload has grown with each decade. Its ability to act in a legitimate, and not just lawful, fashion, beyond the text of the Statute, is key to the achievement of its aims. The previous chapters in this book focused on the problem of asserting authority in the context of free, liberal societies, in which autonomy is prized. The problems associated with authority at the international level were also challenged by the foundation of the system on consensus. The postcolonial context, and the impact of colonialism more generally, also complicates the question of authority, where noble concepts such as civilisation were used as a justification for the brutalisation and exploitation of populations. This makes the task of delineating authority difficult, although not impossible. The exercise of power by the ICC, and by international criminal law more broadly, must focus on the service of justice for victims. Any deviation therefrom will mean that the acts lack legitimacy and would be reduced to exercises of power. Characterising authority as justice is much less utopian than the language may suggest; there is the addition of a practical, and one may argue, necessarily so, dimension to the Court's work. It also has implications for several aspects of the Court's work.

In the first instance, it offers a description of authority which is rooted in neither State consent nor the UN Charter. This is critical because of the postcolonial context, as well as the issue of State consent at the international level. In the second instance, characterising authority as justice focuses on the purposes of the ICC and, by default, international criminal law more broadly. Finally, it honours the history of the discipline, which was rooted in accountability for atrocities. The trial of alleged perpetrators offers a clear and public demonstration of accountability and can be met through the deployment of two key mechanisms: UNSC referrals and the doctrine of complementarity.

Deriving authority from State consent and the UN Charter alone actively undermines the authority of international criminal law because those which fund the Court, and which created the first international criminal tribunals, were the same States which caused enormous harm through colonialism. Consequently, it is too easy, albeit simplistic, to argue that international criminal law is fundamentally a neo-colonial project. A move away from the reliance on State consent, and the proxy of the UN Charter, would allow international criminal law to be justified without any recourse to States. Instead, it provides a coherent, internal logic which supports justice for those who have been victimised by serious violations of international criminal law and avoids the argument, particularly by those who do not wish to be prosecuted for well-evidenced abuses of power, that the Court is a neo-colonial endeavour. The conscious focus on authority as justice requires such individuals to answer to the question of justice and leads on, neatly, to the idea of complementarity. Where authority is derived from justice, the Court may move beyond international prosecution and focus more keenly on the domestic context. This includes examining ways of supporting domestic prosecutions in countries which have been destabilised by war. Equally, a more even-handed approach to examinations and investigations, particularly as watching briefs, would undermine the idea that the Court is focused on Africa and instead would support the idea that it is focused on victims of atrocities around the world. States which have the capacity for prosecution should be supported domestically, as there is no need to elevate every prosecution to the international level.

The mechanism for UNSC referrals has not been used extensively thus far; attempted referrals, such as that for Syria, have been blocked by certain members of the permanent five because of political concerns. This demonstrates the limited authority that States, State consent, and the UN can have in certain situations, if the ultimate determinant is that of power politics. Such exercises are not in keeping with several definitions of authority and undoubtedly lack the focus on justice that the authority of international criminal law ought to have. Accordingly, referrals could have the effect of undermining the Court more than such a mechanism may support its aims; a more active approach to complementarity could, over time, replace the referral mechanism. It would also support the idea, truly, that the authority of international criminal law is rooted completely in justice for the victims.

References

Abass, Ademola, 'The Proposed International Criminal Jurisdiction for the African Court: Some Problematical Aspects' (2013) 60 NILR 27.

Abebe, Zekarias Beshah, 'The African Court with a Criminal Jurisdiction and the ICC: A Case for Overlapping Jurisdiction' (2017) 25 AJICL 418.

Akande, Dapo, 'The Legal Nature of Security Council Referrals to the ICC and Its Impact on Al-Bashir's Immunities' (2009) 7 JICJ 333.

Alter, Karen, *The European Court's Political Power* (Oxford University Press 2009).

The New Terrain of International Courts: Courts, Politics, Rights (Princeton University Press 2014) 4.

Alter, Karen, Helfer, Lawrence and Madsen, Mikael, 'The Variable Authority of International Courts: How Context Shapes the Authority of International Courts' (2016) 79 Law Contemp Probl 1.

International Court Authority (Oxford University Press 2018).

Amann, Diane Marie, 'The Post-Postcolonial Woman or Child' (2015) 30 AUIL 41.

Ambos, Kai, *The Colombian Peace Process and the Principle of Complementarity at the ICC* (Springer 2010).

'Punishment without a Sovereign? The *Ius Puniendi* Issue of International Criminal Law: A First Contribution towards a Consistent Theory of International Criminal Law' (2013) 33 OJLS 293.

Anghie, Antony, *Imperialism, Sovereignty and the Making of International Law* (Cambridge University Press 2005).

Anghie, Antony and Chimni, BS, 'Third World Approaches to International Law and Individual Responsibility in Internal Conflict' (2004) 36 Stud Transnat'l Legal Pol'y 185.

Arendt, Hannah, *Between Past and Future: Six Exercises in Political Thoughts* (Viking 1961) 123.

d'Aspremont, Jean, *Formalism and the Sources of International Law: A Theory of the Ascertainment of Legal Rules* (Oxford University Press 2011).

Austin, John, *The Province of Jurisprudence Determined* (first published 1832, General Books 2012).

Austin, W Chadwick and Thieme, Michael, 'Is the International Criminal Court Anti-African?' (2016) 28 Peace Review 342.

Ba, Oumar, 'International Justice and the Postcolonial Condition' (2017) 63 Africa Today 45.

Baldwin, Clive, 'The ICC Prosecutor Office's Cop-Out on UK Military Crimes in Iraq' *Opinio Juris*, 18 December 2020, http://opiniojuris.org/2020/12/18/the-icc-prosecutor-offices-cop-out-on-uk-military-crimes-in-iraq/.

Bantekas, Ilias, *International Criminal Law* (Hart 2010).

Bassiouni, MC, *The Legislative History of the International Criminal Court* (Ardsley 2005).

'The Permanent International Criminal Court' in M Lattimer and P Sands (eds), *Justice for Crimes against Humanity* (Bloomsbury 2003).

Bekou, Olympia and Cryer, Robert, 'The International Criminal Court and Universal Jurisdiction: A Close Encounter?' (2007) 56 ICLQ 49.

Bennett, Christopher, 'The Authority of Moral Oversight: On the Legitimacy of Criminal Law' (2019) 25 LT 153–177.

Benvenisti, Eyal, 'Sovereigns as Trustees of Humanity: On the Accountability of States to Foreign Stakeholders' (2013) 107 AJIL 295.

von Bernstorff, Jochen, *The Public International Law Theory of Hans Kelsen: Believing in Universal Law* (Cambridge University Press 2010).

'Authority Monism in International Organisations' in Joana Mendes and Ingo Venzke (eds), *Allocating Authority: Who Should Do What in European and International Law?* (Hart 2018) 104.

Besson, Samantha, 'The Authority of International Law: Lifting the State Veil' (2009) 31 Sydney LR 343.

'State Consent and Disagreement in International Law-Making: Dissolving the Paradox' (2016) 29 LJIL 289.

Blome, Kerstin and Makard, Nora, '"Contested Collisions": Conditions for a Successful Collision Management: The Example of Article 16 of the Rome Statute' (2016) 29 LJIL 551.

Bodansky, Daniel, 'The Concept of Legitimacy in International Law' in Rudiger Wolfrum and Volker Roben (eds), *Legitimacy in International Law* (Springer 2008).

Boemeke, Manfred, Feldman, Gerald and Glaser, Elisabeth (eds), *The Treaty of Versailles: A Reassessment after 75 Years* (Cambridge University Press 1998).

Boister, Neil and Cryer, Robert, *The Tokyo International Military Tribunal: A Reappraisal* (Oxford University Press 2008).

Bosco, David, *Rough Justice* (Oxford University Press 2014).

Brehm, Hollie Nyseth, Uggen, Christopher and Gasanabo, Jean-Damascène, 'Genocide, Justice, and Rwanda's Gacaca Courts' (2014) 30 JICJ 333.

Bregman, Rutger, *Humankind: A Hopeful History* (Bloomsbury 2020).

Brolmann, Kiki, 'The PCIJ and International Rights of Group and Individuals' in Christian J Tams and Malgosia Fitzmaurice (eds), *Legacies of the Permanent Court of International Justice* (Martinus Nijhoff 2013).

Buchanan, Allen, *Justice, Legitimacy, and Self-Determination: Moral Foundations for International Law* (Oxford University Press 2003).

'The Legitimacy of International Law' in John Tasioulas and Samantha Besson (eds), *The Philosophy of International Law* (Oxford University Press 2010).

Buchanan, Allen and Keohane, Robert, 'The Legitimacy of Global Governance Institutions' in Lukas H Meyer (ed), *Legitimacy, Justice and Public International Law* (Cambridge University Press 2009).

Butler, Israel de Jesus, 'Securing Human Rights in the Face of International Integration' (2011) 60 ICLQ 125.

Butt, Daniel, 'Victors' Justice? Historic Injustice and the Legitimacy of International Law' in Lukas H Meyer (ed), *Legitimacy, Justice and Public International Law* (Cambridge University Press 2009).

Byers, Michael, *Custom, Power and the Power of Rules* (Cambridge University Press 1999).

Çali, Basak, *The Authority of International Law: Obedience, Respect and Rebuttal* (Oxford University Press 2015).

Callinan, Rory, 'Calls for UK to Investigate Possible War Crimes in Afghanistan' *The Guardian*, 20 November 2020, www.theguardian.com/australia-news/2020/nov/20/calls-for-uk-to-investigate-possible-war-crimes-afghanistan-australian-report.

Carlson, Kerstin Bree, *The Justice Laboratory: International Criminal Justice in Africa* (Brookings Institute 2020).

Caserta, Salvatore, 'Western Centrism, Contemporary International Law, and International Courts' (2021) 34 LJIL 1.

Cassese, Antonio, 'The Legitimacy of International Criminal Tribunals and the Current Prospects of International Criminal Justice' (2012) 25 LJIL 491.

Cassese, Antonio, Acquaviva, Guido G and Fan, Mary De Ming, *International Criminal Law: Cases and Commentary* (Oxford University Press 2011).

Christiano, Thomas, 'Ronald Dworkin, State Consent and Progressive Cosmopolitanism' in Wil Waluchow and Stefan Schiaffra (eds), *The Legacy of Ronald Dworkin* (Oxford University Press 2016).

Clarke, Kamari Maxine, 'Refiguring the Perpetrator: Culpability, History and International Criminal Law's Impunity Gap' (2015) 19 IJHR 592.

Condorelli, Luigi and Ciampi, Annalisa, 'Comments on the UNSC Referral of the Situation in Darfur to the ICC' (2005) 3 JICJ 590.

Cowell, Frederick, 'Inherent Imperialism: Understanding the Legal Roots of Anti-Imperialist Criticism of the International Criminal Court' (2017) 15 JICJ 667.

Crawford, James, *Brownlie's Principles of Public International Law* (Cambridge University Press 2017).

The Creation of States in International Law (2nd edn, Oxford University Press 2006).

Criddle, Evan J and Fox-Decent, Ewan, *Fiduciaries of Humanity: How International Law Constitutes Authority* (Oxford University Press 2016).

Cryer, Robert, 'International Criminal Law vs State Sovereignty: Another Round?' (2005) 16 EJIL 979.

Prosecuting International Crimes (Cambridge University Press 2005).

D'Amato, Anthony, 'On the Legitimacy of International Institutions' in Wil Waluchow and Stefan Schiaffra (eds), *The Legacy of Ronald Dworkin* (Oxford University Press 2016).

Daly, Erin, 'Between Punitive and Reconstructive Justice: The Gacaca Courts in Rwanda' (2001) 34 NYU J Int'l L & Pol 355.

Delmas-Marty, Mireille, 'Interactions between National and International Criminal Law in the Preliminary Phase of Trial at the ICC' (2006) 4 JICJ 2.

Dickinson, Laura A, 'The Promise of Hybrid Courts' (2003) 97 AJIL 295.

Dugard, John, 'Palestine and the International Criminal Court: Institutional Failure or Bias' (2013) 11 JICJ 563.

'Duterte Threatens to Arrest International Criminal Court Prosecutor' *The Guardian*, 13 April 2018.

Dworkin, Ronald M, 'Is Law a System of Rules?' in Ronald M Dworkin (ed), *The Philosophy of Law* (Oxford University Press 1977).

El-Zeidy, Mohammed, 'The Gravity Threshold under the Statute of the International Criminal Court' (2008) 19 CLF 35.

Finnemore, Martha and Goldstein, Judith, 'Power Politics in the Contemporary World: Lessons from the Scholarship of Stephen Krasner' in Martha Finnemore and Judith Goldstein (eds), *Back to Basics: State Power in a Contemporary World* (Oxford University Press 2013).

Fox-Decent, Evan, *Sovereignty's Promise: The State as Fiduciary* (Oxford University Press 2011).

Franck, Thomas, *The Power of Legitimacy among Nations* (Oxford University Press 1990).

'Why a Quest for Legitimacy?' (1987) 21 UC Davis L Rev 535.

Friedman, Lawrence, *The Republic of Choice: Law, Authority and Culture* (Harvard University Press 1990).

Gegout, Catherine, 'The International Criminal Court: Limits, Potential and Conditions for the Promotion of Justice and Peace' (2013) 34 TWQ 800.

Goldman, David B, *Globalisation and the Western Legal Tradition: Recurring Patterns of Law and Authority* (Cambridge University Press 2007).

Gondi, James, 'Debunking the Conspiracy Theory: Analysing the Failure to Achieve Complementarity and the Responsibility to Protect in Kenya and Other Jurisdictions' in Steve Ndirangu, Edigah Kavulavu and Terry Jeff Odhiambo (eds), *International Criminal Justice: The ICC and Complementarity* (ICJ Kenya 2014).

Gregory, Gordon, 'The Trial of Peter von Hagenbach' in Kevin Heller and Gerry Simpson (eds), *The Hidden Histories of War Crimes Trials* (Oxford University Press 2013).

Grotius, Hugo, *Commentary on the Law of Prize and Booty* (Oxford University Press 1950).

The Rights of War and Peace (Liberty Fund 2005).

Guzman, Andrew, 'A Compliance-Based Theory of International Law' (2002) 90 Cal L Rev 1823.

Hall, Stephen, 'The Persistent Spectre: Natural Law, International Order and the Limits of Positivism' (2001) 12 EJIL 269.

Harries, Jill D, 'Resolving Disputes: The Frontiers of Law in Late Antiquity' in Ralph W Mathisen (ed), *Law, Society, and Authority in Late Antiquity* (Oxford University Press 2001).

Hart, HLA, 'Separation of Law and Morals' in Ronald M Dworkin (ed), *The Philosophy of Law* (Oxford University Press 1977).

Hassanein, Ahmed Samir, 'Self-referral of Situations to the International Criminal Court: Complementarity in Practice – Complementarity in Crisis' (2017) 17 ICLR 107.

Hayashi, Nobuo and Baillet, Cecilia, *The Legitimacy of International Criminal Tribunals* (Cambridge University Press 2017).

Helfer, Lawrence R and Showalter, Anne E, 'Opposing International Justice: Kenya's Integrated Backlash Strategy against the ICC' (2017) 17 ICLR 1.

Heller, Kevin Jon, 'The Comoros Declination – and Remarkable Footnote 20' *Opinio Juris*, 4 December 2019.

'The Nine Words that (Wrongly) Doomed the Iraq Investigation' *Opinio Juris*, 10 December 2020.

'The Shadow Side of Complementarity: The Effect of Article 17 of the Rome Statute on National due Process' (2006) 17 CLF 255.

Higgins, Rosalyn, 'Thinking about the Individual in International Law' (1978) 4 BJIS 1.

'ICC – 20th Anniversary of the Rome Statute' *France Diplomacy*, 17 July 2018.

'ICC debate: Africa vs 'Infamous Caucasian Court'?' *Al-Jazeera*, 28 October 2016. www.aljazeera.com/news/2016/10/28/icc-debate-africa-vs-infamous-caucasian-court.

'IHAT to Close at the End of June' UK Ministry of Defence, 5 April 2017.

Imoedemhe, Ovo, 'Unpacking the Tension between the African Union and the International Criminal Court: The Way Forward' (2015) 23 AJICL 74.

Jalloh, Charles Chernor, 'Regionalizing International Criminal Law' (2009) 9 ICLR 445.

Jayasuriya, Kanishka, *Reconstituting the Global Liberal Order: Legitimacy, Regulation and Security* (Routledge 2005).

Kammerhofer, Jorg, *Uncertainty in International Law: A Kelsenian Perspective* (Routledge 2011).

Kant, Immanuel, *Perpetual Peace* (first published 1795, Hackett 2003).

Katzenstein, Peter J, 'States and Power as Ur-Force: Domestic Traditions and Embedded Actors in World Politics' in Martha Finnemore and Judith Goldstein (eds), *Back to Basics: State Power in a Contemporary World* (Oxford University Press 2013).

Kaul, HansPeter, 'The Nuremberg Legacy and the International Criminal Court: Lecture in Honor of Whitney R. Harris, former Nuremberg Prosecutor' (2013) 12 WUGSLR 637.

Kelsen, Hans, *Pure Theory of Law* (2nd edn, The Lawbook Exchange 2005).

'Kenneth Roth's Statement at the Commemoration of the 20th Anniversary of the Adoption of the Rome Statute of the International Criminal Court' *Human Rights Watch*, 17 July 2018.

Kirkby, Coel, 'Rwanda's Gacaca Courts: A Preliminary Critique' (2006) 2 JAL 94.

Kiyani, Asad G, 'Third World Approaches to International Criminal Law' (2016) 109 AJIL Unbound 255, 258.

'The Three Dimensions of Selectivity in International Criminal Law' (2017) 15 JICJ 624.

Kjeldgaard-Pedersen, Astrid, 'What Defines an International Criminal Court? A Critical Assessment of "the Involvement of the International Community"' (2015) 28 LJIL 113.

Kleinlein, Thomas, 'On Holism, Pluralism, and Democracy: Approaches to Constitutionalism beyond the State' (2010) 21 EJIL 1075.

Koh, Harold Hongju, 'Why Do Nations Obey International Law?' (1997) 106 Yale LJ 2599, 2652.

Kolb, Robert, 'Discussion of TH Cheng's Monograph When International Law Work, and in Particular a Defence of the Nicaragua Judgment of the ICJ' (2013) 26 LJIL 751.

Koskenniemi, Martti, *From Apology to Utopia* (Cambridge University Press 2006).

'International Law and Empire, Aspects and Approaches' in Martti Koskinniemi, Walter Rech and Manuel Jiminez Fonseca (eds), *International Law and Empire* (Cambridge University Press 2017).

Krasner, Stephen, 'New Terrains: Sovereignty and Alternative Conceptions of Power' in Martha Finnemore and Judith Goldstein (eds), *Back to Basics: State Power in a Contemporary World* (Oxford University Press 2013).

Kumm, Mattias, 'The Legitimacy of International Law: A Constitutionalist Framework of Analysis' (2004) 15 EJIL 907.

Lacey, Marc, 'A Decade after Massacres, Rwanda Outlaws Ethnicity' *The New York Times*, 9 April 2004. www.nytimes.com/2004/04/09/world/a-decade-after-massacres-rwanda-outlaws-ethnicity.html.

Lake, David A, 'Authority, Coercion and Power in International Relations' in Martha Finnemore and Judith Goldstein (eds), *Back to Basics: State Power in a Contemporary World* (Oxford University Press 2013).

Lang, Arabella, 'Iraq Historic Allegations Team' HC Briefing Paper 7478 22 January 2016.

Langer, Maximo and Mackenzie, Eason, 'The Quiet Expansion of Universal Jurisdiction' (2019) 30(3) EJIL 779.

Lee, Roy (ed), *The International Criminal Court: The Making of the Rome Statute* (Kluwer Law International 1999).

'Libya: Words to Deeds: The Urgent Need for Human Rights Reform' (2006) 18 Human Rights Watch 1E.

Luban, David, 'Fairness to Rights: Jurisdiction, Legality and the Legitimacy of International Criminal Law' in John Tasioulas and Samantha Besson (eds), *The Philosophy of International Law* (Oxford University Press 2010).

May, Thomas, *Autonomy, Authority and Moral Responsibility* (Springer 1998).

McGoldrick, Dominic, 'The International Criminal Court: An End to Impunity?' (1999) 8 CLR 627.

McGuinness, Margaret E, 'Peace v. Justice: The Universal Declaration of Human Rights and the Modern Origins of the Debate' (2011) 35 Dip His 749.

Mégrét, Frédéric, 'From "Savages" to "Unlawful Combatants": A Postcolonial Look at International Humanitarian Law's "Other"' in Anne Orford (ed), *International Law and Its Others* (Cambridge University Press 2006).

Mégret, Frédéric and Giles Samson, Marika, 'Holding the Line on Complementarity in Libya: The Case for Tolerating Flawed Domestic Trials' (2013) 11 JICJ 571.

Mattes, Hanspeter, 'Libya since 2011: Political Transformation and Violence' (2016) 23 Middle East Policy 59.

Mettraux, Guénaël (ed), *Perspectives on the Nuremberg Trial* (Oxford University Press 2008).

Meyer, Lukas and Sanklecha, Pranay, 'Three Perspectives on the Debate' in Lukas H Meyer (ed), *Legitimacy, Justice and Public International Law* (Cambridge University Press 2009).

Milanovic, Marko, 'Is the Rome Statute Binding on Individuals?' (2011) 9 JICJ 25.

Mill, John Stuart, *On Liberty* (first published 1859, Dover Publications 2002).
Mutua, Makau wa, 'Why Redraw the Map of Africa: A Moral and Legal Inquiry' (1995) 16 MJIL 1113.
Nagel, Thomas, 'Moral Conflict and Political Legitimacy' in Joseph Raz (ed), *Authority* (Basil Blackwell 1990).
Nault, Derrick M, *Africa and the Shaping of International Human Rights* (Oxford University Press 2020).
Nesiah, Vasuki, 'Placing International Law: White Spaces on a Map' (2003) 16 LJIL 1.
Niang, Mandiaye, 'Africa and the Legitimacy of the ICC in Question' (2017) 17 ICLR 615.
Nsereko, Daniel, 'The ICC and Complementarity in Principle' (2013) 26 LJIL 427.
O'Connell, Mary Ellen, *The Power and Purpose of International Law: Insights from the Theory and Practice of Enforcement* (Oxford University Press 2008).
Oppenheim, Lassa, *International Law: A Treatise – vol 2: Peace* (2nd edn, Longman 1912).
Papillon, Sophie, 'Has the United Nations Security Council Implicitly Removed Al-Bashir's Immunity?' (2010) 10 ICLR 275.
Paulson, Stanley, 'Classical Legal Positivism at Nuremberg' (1975) 4 Phil & PA 132–158.
Pellet, Alain, 'Legitimacy of Legislative and Executive Actions of International Institutions' in Wil Waluchow and Stefan Schiaffra (eds), *The Legacy of Ronald Dworkin* (Oxford University Press 2016).
Pinto Soares, Patricia, 'Positive Complementarity and the Law Enforcement Network: Drawing Lessons from the Ad Hoc Tribunals' Completion Strategy' (2013) 46 ILR 319, 323.
Plotnitsky, Arkady, *Nils Bohr and Complementarity. An Introduction* (Springer 2012).
Prosecuting Putin for His Crime of Aggression against Ukraine: Part One | OHRH (ox.ac.uk).
al-Qaddafi, Muammar, *Green Book* (Medina University Press 2021).
Rasiah, Nathan, 'The Court Martial of Corporal Payne and Others and the Future Landscape of International Criminal Justice' (2009) 7 JICJ 177.
Raymond, Gregory A, 'Problems and Prospects in the Study of International Norms' (1997) 41 MISR 205.
Raz, Joseph (ed), *Authority* (Basil Blackwell 1990).
Raz, Joseph, 'Authority and Justification' in Joseph Raz (ed) *Authority* (Basil Blackwell 1990).
The Authority of Law (1st edn, Oxford University Press 1979).
Between Authority and Interpretation: On the Theory of Law and Practical Reason (Oxford University Press 2009).
The Morality of Freedom (Oxford University Press 1988).
Reisinger Coracini, Astrid, 'Amended Most Serious Crimes: A New Category of Core Crimes within the Jurisdiction but Out of the Reach of the International Criminal Court?' (2008) 21 LJIL 699.
Report on the Baha Mousa Public Inquiry, Volumes 1–3, HC 1452 2011–12, 8 September 2011.
Report of the Inquiry into Allegations against the Security Forces of Physical Brutality in Northern Ireland Arising Out of Events on the 9th August, 1971.

Report of Inquiry under Division 4A of Part 4 of the Inspector-General of the Australian Defence Force Regulation 2016 into Questions of Unlawful Conduct Concerning the Special Operations Task Group in Afghanistan, 10 November 2020.

Report of the Iraq Inquiry HC 264, July 2016.

Report on Preliminary Examinations 2011, 13 December 2011, Office of the Prosecutor.

Report on Preliminary Examination Activities 2020 (Colombia), 14 December 2020, Office of the Prosecutor.

Report on the Situation in the Republic of Korea: Article 5 Report, June 2014, Office of the Prosecutor.

Report on the Situation in Iraq/UK Final Report, Office of the Prosecutor, 9 December 2020.

Reynolds, John and Xavier, Sujith, 'The Dark Corners of the World' (2016) 14 JICJ 959.

Robinson, Darryl, 'Inescapable Dyads: Why the International Criminal Court Cannot Win' (2015) 28 LJIL 323.

Roper, Steven and Barria, Lilian, 'State Cooperation and International Criminal Court Bargaining Influence in the Arrest and Surrender of Suspects' (2008) 21 LJIL 457.

Roughan, Nicole, *Authorities: Conflicts, Cooperation and Transnational Legal Theories* (Oxford University Press 2013).

Rudolf, Christopher, *Power and Principle* (Cornell University Press 2017).

Russian Invasion of Ukraine, 'Ukraine War in Maps: Tracking the Russian Invasion' BBC News.

Sacouto, Susana, and Cleary, Katherine, 'The Katanga Complementarity Decisions: Sound Law but Flawed Policy' (2010) 23 LJIL 363.

Sands, Philippe, *Lawless Word: Making and Breaking Global Rules* (Penguin 2006).

Schabas, William, *The Cambridge Companion to International Criminal Law* (Cambridge University Press 2015).

'Complementarity in Practice: Some Uncomplimentary Thoughts' (2008) 19 CLF 5.

The International Criminal Court: A Commentary on the Rome Statute (Oxford University Press 2010).

'Victor's Justice: Selecting "Situations" at the International Criminal Court' (2010) 43 JMLR 535.

Scharf, Michael P, 'International Law and the Torture Memos' (2009) 42 Case W Res J Int'l L 321.

Scheipers, Sibylle, *Negotiating Sovereignty and Human Rights: International Society and the International Criminal Court* (Manchester University Press 2012).

Scott, Shirley V, 'International Law as Ideology: Theorizing the Relationship between International Law and International Politics' (1994) 5 EJIL 313.

Sellars, Kirsten, 'Imperfect Justice at Nuremberg and Tokyo' (2010) 21 EJIL 1085–1102.

Shapiro, Scott, 'Authority' in Jules Coleman and Scott Shapiro (eds), *The Oxford Handbook of Jurisprudence and the Philosophy of Law* (Oxford University Press 2002).

Smith, David, 'New Chief Prosecutor Defends International Criminal Court' *The Guardian*, 23 May 2012.

Smith, RW, 'The Concept of Legitimacy' (1970) 35 Theoria 17.

Spaventa, Eleanor, 'Opening Pandora's Box: Some Reflections on the Constitutional Effects of the Decision in Pupino' (2007) 3 ECLR 5.

Stahn, Carsten, 'A Tale of Two Notions of Complementarity' (2008) 19 CLF 87.

Stillmann, Peter, 'A Concept of Legitimacy' (1974) 7 Polity 32.

'Sudan: Reaction to Warrant for Bashir's Arrest' *Thomson Reuters*, 4 March 2009.

'Sudanese President Tells International Criminal Court to "Eat the Arrest Warrant"' *The Guardian*, 4 March 2009. www.theguardian.com/world/2009/mar/04/sudan-al-bashir-war-crimes.

Sukharev, Alexander, 'The Nuremberg Tribunal and the Problems of International Rule of Law' (2006) 77 RIDP 711.

Teitel, Ruti, *Humanity's Law* (Oxford University Press 2011).

Tiemessen, Alana, 'The International Criminal Court and the Politics of Prosecutions (2014) 18 IJHR 444.

Totani, Yuma, *The Tokyo War Crimes Trial: The Pursuit of Justice in the Wake of World War II* (Harvard University Press 2009).

Triffterer, Otto (ed), *Commentary on the Rome Statute of the International Criminal Court* (Beck Hart Nomos 2008).

Van Mulligen, Johannes Gerald, 'Global Constitutionalism and the Objective Purport of the International Legal Order' (2011) 24 LJIL 277.

van Roermund, Bert, 'Instituting Authority: Some Kelsenian Notes' (2002) 15 RJ 206.

Vinjamuri, Leslie, 'The International Criminal Court and the Paradox of Authority' in Karen J Alter, Laurence R Helfer and Mikael Rask Madsen (eds), 'The Variable Authority of International Courts: How Context Shapes the Authority of International Courts' (2016) 79 Law Contemp Probl 1.

Verini, James, 'The Prosecutor and the President' *New York Times Magazine*, 22 June 2016.

Vitoria, Francisco (ed AR Pagden and Jeremy Lawrance), *Vitoria: Political Writings* (Cambridge University Press 1991)

Weber, Max, 'The Three Types of Legitimate Rule' (1958) 4 Berkeley Pub Soc Inst 1.

Wheatley, Steven, 'A Democratic Rule of International Law' (2011) 22 EJIL 525, 532–533.

Wieczorek, Irene, *The Legitimacy of EU Criminal Law* (Hart 2020).

de Wijk, Rob, *Power Politics: How China and Russia Reshape the World* (Amsterdam University Press 2015).

Wolff, RP, The Conflict between Authority and Autonomy, in Joseph Raz (ed), *Authority* (Basil Blackwell 1990).

Wright, Quincy, 'The Proposal for an International Criminal Court' (1952) 46 AJIL 60.

Index

For EU product safety concerns, contact us at Calle de José Abascal, 56–1°, 28003 Madrid, Spain or eugpsr@cambridge.org.

www.ingramcontent.com/pod-product-compliance
Lightning Source LLC
LaVergne TN
LVHW011815200926
848484LV00005B/1211

* 9 7 8 1 1 0 8 4 8 3 6 5 0 *